PAUL
OF TARSUS

www.realreads.co.uk

Retold by Alan Moore and Gill Tavner
Illustrated by Karen Donnelly

Published by Real Reads Ltd
Stroud, Gloucestershire, UK
www.realreads.co.uk

First published in 2010

ISBN 978-1-906230-29-6

Printed in China by Imago Ltd
Designed by Lucy Guenot
Typeset by Bookcraft Ltd, Stroud, Gloucestershire

CONTENTS

THE CHARACTERS

Saul/Paul

Saul is determined to crush the 'Jesus movement'. Later, renamed Paul, he spreads the news of Jesus around the world. What happened to change him?

Simon Peter

Jesus's loyal disciple is now a leader in the growing church. Will he and Paul ever reach agreement?

Barnabas

Barnabas leads Paul to Jesus's friends. What further role will he play in Paul's work?

Ananias

Ananias lives in Damascus. What role does God want him to play in his plans for Saul?

James

James is Jesus's brother and a leader in the growing church. Can he and Paul find a way to work together?

Timothy

Timothy hears Paul preach in Lystra, and decides to help him. What will his role be?

Silas

When Silas joins Paul in Antioch, does he know that it's just the beginning of a very long journey?

PAUL OF TARSUS

This imprisonment has lasted so long, compressing my energy until the pressure feels so immense that the walls should blast apart. I need to be out there. There's so much still to do, half the world still to visit. How can I do God's work from here? I might not have much time left. I need to focus. Think, Paul, think.

People say the letters I've written during my life have been more powerful than my spoken words, but the guards won't let me send any more. Perhaps I should write an account of my life and hide it so that one day it might be found, and help people in centuries to come to understand the good news of Jesus Christ.

But can I remember all the journeys? Can I remember the people I met, the words I wrote? Will I have time? With God's grace, I will try.

My parents named me Saul. I was brought up as a Jew and as a Roman citizen in Tarsus, far from the Jewish homeland. It wasn't easy being Jewish in a Gentile society. As a minority we felt that we had to assert our identity, deliberately setting ourselves apart as God's people by strict adherence to the laws passed to us by Moses. I remember many arguments when I tried to explain to non-believers the things that made my Jewish faith so special. Perhaps adversity made us stronger, more rigid in our beliefs.

I've never been a man to do things by halves. If I believe something then I believe it with every part of my being, and I have to act upon it. I believed in the Jewish law – the Torah – and therefore I wanted to teach and enforce it. As soon as I was old enough, I travelled to Jerusalem to study to be a Pharisee.

I had a full classical education, but now I needed to concentrate on the Torah. My fervour and energy were soon noticed by the Supreme

Jewish Council – the Sanhedrin. They placed
considerable authority upon my young shoulders.
I loved it. I was determined that nothing should
dilute or weaken the Jewish faith.

I became increasingly aware of a movement of
people developing around a man called Jesus.
I hadn't met Jesus, but I heard about him with
concern. Although Jewish himself, Jesus was

challenging our laws, sometimes openly breaking them and claiming that he had God's authority to do so. Some people said that he was the Son of God, some even claimed that he was God. This was outrageous, or so I thought at the time.

I was relieved when the Romans nailed Jesus to a wooden cross. I thought it would remove the threat he posed to Jewish unity. However, within weeks I realised that his death posed an even greater problem than his life. Stories of him rising from the dead circulated rapidly. People even claimed to have seen him. This, they said, proved that he was the Son of God, and that he had died so that our sins would be forgiven.

I refused to believe such nonsense. Not only had Jesus undermined the Torah during his lifetime, but his death by crucifixion was shameful. Jewish law teaches that anyone who dies on a tree is cursed. What would Gentiles think about Jews if we worshipped a God who allowed his own son to die in such a cursed way?

Even worse – if Jesus *was* the Son of God, we had helped the Romans to subject our God to an agonising death. We were supposed to be a light to the nations; this would make us a laughing stock.

So while Jesus's life was a problem for us, his death was a major stumbling block. The Jesus movement had to be stopped. These people wouldn't be reasoned out of their beliefs; in fact, they were prepared to die for them. While I admired this single-mindedness, indeed recognised it within myself, I had to do what was necessary. If death was the only way to stop them, they must die.

I soon gained a reputation for the brutal persecution of Jesus's followers. My name became fearful to them. My determined efforts

steadily enabled many synagogues to return to
the uninterrupted teaching of the Torah. When I
learned that Jesus's followers were preaching in
the city of Damascus, I gained the Sanhedrin's
permission to travel there and arrest them. I set
out urgently that same day with a group of loyal
men. Little could I have guessed where that road
to Damascus would lead me.

At first it was a journey like any other but, as I was striding along the dusty road, a sudden blinding light, pure, brilliant white, brought me to my knees. Rather than illuminating, the light burned away my vision. Within the light I heard a voice, 'Saul, Saul, why do you persecute me?'

'Who are you?' I asked.

'I am Jesus, the man you are persecuting. Get up, go to Damascus. You will be told what to do.'

The light left me blind. My men helped me to my feet and led me into the city. For three days I was unable to eat or drink. I experienced more visions of Jesus. On the third day, I had a visitor. The man placed his trembling hands upon my shoulders. 'Brother Saul, I am Ananias. The Lord Jesus has sent me to restore your sight so that you may be filled with the Holy Spirit.'

Days earlier, I had met the risen Jesus. Now I witnessed the wonder of his power. Without a doubt, Jesus Christ was the Son of God. Ananias baptised me. At once, my sight returned and the Holy Spirit entered my heart. As I said, I've never been a man to do things by halves.

This was immense! I understood that Jesus had died and risen again so that we can start anew with God. *This* was the good news that I had to tell everyone about! That very day I began to teach that the Torah would not lead people to God. Only Jesus can do that.

The people I had come to Damascus to arrest offered me cautious hospitality – it must have been difficult to trust me. Most other Jews were furious. They had expected me to remove the threat; instead I was strengthening it. Now it was me that had to be stopped.

I travelled to Arabia. I needed to spread my message, and to learn all that I could about Jesus.

My name – Saul – troubled me. Saul, the first King of Israel, had done terrible things. Like him, I had made Saul a name to be feared. Besides, as Jesus's message wasn't only for Jews, I needed a less Jewish, more Romanised name. The name Paul means 'small' and, as I'm quite a small man, it seemed appropriate.

After an absence of nearly three years I briefly returned to Damascus. I now had a stronger message, and although

some people accepted it, many others rejected it angrily. Eventually the situation became so tense that some of my friends had to help me to escape by lowering me from the city walls in a basket.

For the first time since my conversion, I travelled to Jerusalem. I wondered whether I would meet the people who had known Jesus during his lifetime. I knew they would find it difficult to trust me. I didn't really mind whether I met them or not – my own knowledge of Jesus was already sufficient – but I was interested enough to allow a man called Barnabas to lead me to them.

At first it was awkward, but they put their faith in God. 'Stay with me,' offered Simon Peter, a man who had been very close to Jesus. 'I have many stories to tell you.'

Not all Jews in Jerusalem were so welcoming. As in Damascus, many were furious that I was preaching about Jesus instead of enforcing the Torah. I wasn't afraid of their fury. When I felt that I had completed my work in Jerusalem, I returned to Tarsus to prepare for the future.

Four years passed before I met Barnabas again. Having heard that I was spreading the good news about Jesus amongst both Jews and non-Jews, he came to Tarsus to seek my help. 'The Greeks in Antioch are responding well,' he explained. 'Will you come and help me?'

'Barnabas, just as you introduced me to the Jerusalem brethren, you must introduce me to the new followers in Antioch. Of course I will help you.'

Antioch now became my base. The number of believers there increased to such an extent that we gained our own identity – Christians, people called us; followers of Christ. After my first year there a famine struck Judea, causing great suffering in Jerusalem. Christians in Antioch wanted to send food to relieve the brethren in Jerusalem. Barnabas and I delivered it, then returned to Antioch.

I felt driven to teach about Jesus in as many lands as I could possibly reach. Accompanied by Barnabas and his nephew, John Mark, I sailed to Cyprus and then on to the mainland where we taught in many cities.

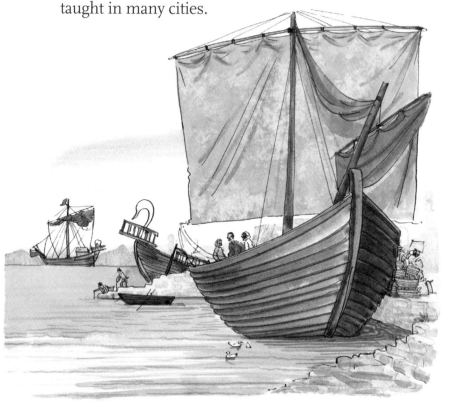

We met with both hostility and friendship.
By the time we returned to Antioch two years
later, we were confident that we had left behind
us thriving communities of people prepared
to live by the teachings of Jesus, who they now
recognised as the Son of God.

We sailed home to a problem. Everywhere I
had taught, I had spoken to Jews and non-Jews
alike, for the news about Jesus is not only for
Jews. Infuriatingly, in my absence, believers
from Jerusalem had been telling Christians in
Antioch that they must first follow the Torah in
order to follow Jesus.

'The law is above all else,' they claimed. I
used to say the same thing myself, but now
I thought very differently. 'The law served us
well until Jesus came, but we don't need it
any more. Jesus is the new way forward for
everybody.'

'But only if they become Jewish first,' they insisted. This endless discussion about whether Christ's followers should first become Jews has dogged me ever since. I stayed in Antioch for three more years, but the argument simply wouldn't go away. Needing to settle it once and for all, Barnabas and I decided to travel to Jerusalem to discuss it with Simon Peter and the other disciples.

Jesus's brother, James, chaired the discussion. It sometimes angers me that those who knew Jesus during his lifetime assume superiority. Like them, I have met the risen Christ. Through many visions he has taught me all I need to know. My relationship with Jesus is just as personal as theirs.

After a long and heated debate, James agreed with me. We returned to Antioch with a letter from James saying clearly that people didn't have to become Jewish in order to follow Jesus. James told me to continue preaching to Gentiles, while the Jerusalem brethren would preach to the Jews. His only other instruction was that we should continue to help the poor. With my mission clarified, I was ready to set sail again.

This time I was more ambitious. As well as revisiting the people I had already converted, I planned to travel further afield. Unfortunately, my plans were thrown at the last minute by Barnabas. He wanted to bring his nephew John Mark again, but I felt that John had let us down last time.

'Then I can't sail with you,' declared Barnabas.

I would have liked Barnabas's company, but I wouldn't compromise. Instead I took Silas, a good man who had returned with us from Jerusalem to Antioch. He would be a powerful speaker. Barnabas and I parted, and I had a new travelling companion.

At first our journey took us to places I had visited before, and I was pleased to see that communities were still strong in their belief in Jesus. In Lystra we met Timothy, who joined us in our work, and so we became three – Silas, Timothy and me – united in our determination to carry the news about Jesus to as many places as possible.

This was no easy task. We were chased from some towns, beaten in others, and in Philippi we were put in prison, but we were never afraid. In Galatia our progress stalled when I became ill, but the people welcomed us and cared for me. My illness was God's way of keeping us in Galatia long enough to carry out his work.

Later we worked among the people of Thessalonia in Greece. We didn't seek praise, because our words were God's, not our own. In order not to be a burden to the people we stayed with I earned money by working with leather and canvas. We did, however, accept donations to support the brethren in Jerusalem. We grew to love the people we met. We taught that Jesus's death allowed a new start for us all. We taught them how to deserve God's love.

We didn't try to avoid the rougher, more difficult cities. Corinth was a cosmopolitan sea port, well

known for the immoral ways of its people. Many
Corinthians were preoccupied with status, judging
each other by wealth and power rather than by
goodness and kindness. The Holy Spirit worked
through us, and in spite of the difficulties many
Corinthians were baptised in Jesus's name. We
were helped by Priscilla and Aquila, a very able
Jewish couple who had been exiled from Rome by
the Emperor Claudius. When we left Corinth, they
came with us.

Whenever we left a town I felt great concern for the Christians we left behind. They faced fierce opposition and great dangers. I often wondered whether their new beliefs were strong enough. While I was busy in Athens, I sent Timothy back to Thessalonia because I was concerned about my people there. When he returned, he reassured me that they were standing firm in the Lord. I longed to visit them.

'Write them a letter,' suggested Timothy.

Grace and peace to the church of the Thessalonians from Paul, Silas and Timothy.

We thank God for you in our prayers, remembering your faith, love and hard work.

I have been worried that you might have forgotten what we taught you, but Timothy has returned to tell me that you are standing firm in God's love. I hope to visit you soon and strengthen you.

The time of Jesus's return will come suddenly, without warning, like a thief in the night. But don't worry – you won't be taken by surprise because you have heard the word of God, you live in the light. These are brutal times, but when Jesus comes he will save all of us who live and die for him, so that we will be with him forever.

Be ready. Be self-controlled. Protect yourselves with the hope of being saved by Jesus who died for us, so that we will live together with him.

I hear that you are living in a way that will please God. Continue like this. We don't need to write to you about brotherly love because we know that you love your neighbours throughout Macedonia. Build upon this.

Live quietly, mind your own business, work with your hands so that your work will be respected by others. Respect people who work hard and warn those who are lazy. Encourage the timid, help the weak, and be patient with everyone. Never seek revenge; be kind to all; be joyful always. Pray and give thanks. Don't discourage people or put out the spirit's fire, but listen to the truth.

May the God of peace keep you holy and may you be found blameless when the time comes.

Pray for us. The grace of Jesus Christ be with you.

Corinth was more difficult. In such a cosmopolitan city, where new ideas constantly challenged the old, it was difficult to convince people that the good news about Jesus was all they needed. After eighteen months there, although we made great progress, I left with an anxious heart.

We travelled slowly towards Jerusalem. Priscilla and Aquila agreed to stay in Ephesus where we felt they could be very effective. Eventually, Silas, Timothy and I returned to Antioch – to more trouble.

The argument about whether Christians needed to follow Jewish law was still raging. Simon Peter visited us from Jerusalem. The Torah forbids Jews from mixing with Gentiles, but we persuaded Simon Peter to ignore this and dine with us. After all, he had seen Jesus do the same.

Other Christians, brethren who were also Jews, arrived from Jerusalem, and I noticed Simon Peter withdraw from the company of Gentiles. Even Barnabas, who had led many Gentiles to Christ, withdrew from our table.

I was disappointed and angry. How many times did I have to explain that Jesus's death and resurrection changed everything? 'Jesus gave us a new start in our relationship with God,' I argued. 'The Torah isn't necessary now – all we need is faith in Jesus.'

Still Simon Peter stayed away. I had to confront him. 'Before these people came from Jerusalem you ate with Gentiles. You are a hypocrite, Simon Peter!' I could see he still thought he was right.

It wasn't only in Antioch that the brethren were making their influence felt. They were visiting lands in which I had taught about Jesus and undoing my work. I was particularly upset that they visited the Galatians, who had cared for me in my illness. 'Paul preaches falsehoods,' the visitors accused. 'He casts

aside the Torah to make it easier for him to convert people. We knew the living Jesus. Paul didn't.'
The worst part of it was that the Galatians listened. They began to doubt what I had taught them.

Grace and peace to the church of the Galatians from Paul, an apostle sent by Jesus Christ.

I am astonished that you have forgotten the good news so quickly! Some people are confusing you about Jesus Christ. Their news is false. The news I teach was given to me by Jesus himself.

You know that God revealed his son to me. You know that James and Simon Peter agreed that I should preach to Gentiles. They didn't even insist that Titus, a Greek, should become Jewish before he could be a Christian.

You foolish Galatians! Who has bewitched you?
I write in a heavy hand because I am angry. You welcomed Christ, who teaches that there is no difference between Jew and Greek, between slave and free, between male and female, because we are all equal in his eyes. All that counts is faith working through love.

You received the Holy Spirit by hearing about Christ, not through the Torah. God sent his son to free us, but you are in danger of becoming slaves to the Torah. Is this what you want – to be slaves? If you become slaves to the law, Christ will be of no value to you.

The law can be summed up in one command – love your neighbour. If you insist on being slaves, be slaves in service to each other. Help each other all you can, and take pride only in your good actions. Do not allow self-indulgence and lack of self-control to get in the way of your new freedom.

May I never boast of anything except Jesus Christ. Whether you are Jew or Gentile means nothing to me. What counts is a new creation. Peace and mercy to all who follow Jesus.

I needed to follow this letter with a visit to Galatia as soon as possible. After some hurried preparations I left Antioch. Timothy and I travelled through Asia Minor. When we arrived in Galatia I found they had received my letter.

Unconvinced that it had been effective, we left to join Priscilla and Aquilla in Ephesus. Although Christians still faced great dangers there, I saw enough potential to encourage me to stay.

After many months, news reached me from Corinth that my congregations were quarrelling among themselves. It seemed that they had returned to their former concerns with status, wealth, and what they considered to be wisdom. I was deeply distressed. Such divisions would weaken them. I decided to send Timothy with a letter. He would guide them back to Christ.

Grace and peace to the church in Corinth.

I hear that you are arguing, some of you claiming to be followers of Paul, others of Peter. The truth could not be simpler – you are all followers of Christ.

Stop arguing! You don't need law courts to settle your disputes; settle them yourselves with love. Don't take pride in wealth or cleverness. For true wisdom we need the spirit of God, we must be spiritual rather than worldly-wise.

I planted a seed in Corinth, and God made it grow so you are now Christ's servants, and servants of Christ put themselves last. We must be faithful, because our eventual judgement will be by God, not by men. Christ is the head of every person, and the head of Christ is God.

I hear reports of immorality and greed. This is not Christ's way. I understand that even when you gather as a church there are divisions among you. You have misunderstood the purpose of the Lord's Supper, which is a bond between us and

*with Christ; it makes Christ present among us. I
hear that some of you use the Lord's Supper as an
opportunity to feast and get drunk, while others
remain hungry.*

*On the night Jesus was betrayed he told his
disciples to eat the bread and drink the wine
in remembrance of him. It is his body and his
blood. If you eat the bread or drink the cup in
greed and selfishness, you sin against the body of
the Lord.*

*Do not boast of your talents. We have all
been given different spiritual gifts. They go
together to make up one body, the body of Christ.
All parts of the body are necessary. Use your
talents to help each other and to strengthen the
church. Our different gifts, whatever they may be,
are nothing without love.*

*Love is patient and kind, not envious or
boastful. Love isn't proud, rude or self-seeking.
Love is not easily angered, it doesn't bear grudges.
Love doesn't delight in evil; it rejoices in the truth.*

It always protects, trusts, hopes and perseveres. Other gifts will pass away, but love never fails.

When I was a child I thought and talked like a child. As a man, I know many more things, but I still understand little. Only through Jesus Christ shall I reach full understanding, just as he fully understands me. When all other gifts pass away, three things remain: faith, hope, and love. The greatest of these is love.

*Christ died for our sins, was buried and raised again. He appeared to the twelve disciples, then to hundreds of his followers. Then he appeared to me. Jesus **was** raised, and this gives meaning to everything we do. Christ **has** defeated death.*

I will visit you soon. Christians here in Ephesus send you greeting.

My love to all of you in Christ Jesus.

I stayed for three years in Ephesus, but I was anxious to visit my friends in Corinth. How had my letter been received?

I was overjoyed to see my beloved Corinthians again, but though many had taken the words of my letter to heart, some still questioned my authority and criticised my preaching. One particular man insulted me, causing me great pain. An insult to me was an insult to all members of the churches I had founded, so the faithful people punished him. Realising that my presence was causing division, I decided to leave earlier than I had planned.

Timothy and I travelled back through Macedonia. Our next significant stop was in Philippi, where news soon reached us that the Corinthians were sorry for the distress they had caused.

Greetings and comfort to the Church of God in Corinth from Paul and Timothy.

Praise God who, by comforting us in our suffering, teaches us to comfort others. We have endured great hardship and danger in our journeys. We have been beaten, imprisoned, stoned and whipped. This has taught us to rely upon God rather than upon ourselves.

We have always treated you with honesty and holiness. I am sorry that my last visit caused such pain. You have sufficiently punished the man who insulted me; now you should forgive and comfort him.

We know and trust each other, don't we? You are the result of our ministry, which is God's word, not our own. Jesus Christ opens our hearts to God's radiance. I know I am a weak person to carry such a glorious message, but my very weakness proves that the power comes from God alone, not from me.

When our earthly bodies die, we will be judged by Christ who died to free our spirit from our worldly selves. Be reconciled to God. By enduring difficulties, behaving as Christ taught and trying to be faithful, we show ourselves to be servants of God.

My beloved Corinthians, my heart is wide open to you. I would live or die for you. If I caused you sorrow by my last letter and visit, I am sorry for it, but I am happy that it led you back to God.

The Churches of Macedonia have given as much as they are able to the collection for Jerusalem. You should give generously too; your reward will be great. Your giving will not only meet the needs of God's people, but it is an expression of thanks to God.

May the grace of the Lord Jesus Christ and the love of God and the fellowship of the Holy Spirit be with you all.

I've always been a poor speaker, but what I say and do is full of the love of the Lord. When better speakers visit my congregations with different messages, they have a strong impact. This has always worried me, because they don't preach the good news of Christ's death opening our relationship with God. Instead, they usually try to lead my congregations back towards Jewish law.

It was impossible for me to be everywhere at once. As soon as I left a city, others moved into my place to undo my work. I heard that it had happened again in Corinth. As letters were now a crucial part of my ministry, I wrote another to the Corinthians.

From Paul, a true apostle of our Lord Jesus Christ, to the churches of Corinth.

Some of you say that I am timid when with you but bold in my letters, that my letters are weighty but I am a poor speaker. Remember that Christ was both meek and powerful.

Though that may be true, the words I speak have divine power to tear down, destroy and take captive any thoughts or actions levelled against Christ. We don't use the world's weapons; we use gentle weapons to do our work. I am not ashamed to boast of the authority God gave to me. We brought you the good news, and we hope to spread it further.

I don't want my letters to frighten you, but I'm afraid that you will be led astray by better preachers who preach a different Jesus than the one we know. They boast of their abilities, and take from you. Why do you put up with them?

I love you, and Christ, more than they do. I take nothing from you. I have suffered flogging, imprisonment, shipwrecks and dangers, and daily I live with concern for my churches. If you're weak, I feel weak. If you sin, I burn inwardly. I boast of the things that show my weakness because they also show Christ's strength and love. I have often pleaded with God to take away my physical weakness, but he replied, 'My love is enough; my power is made perfect in weakness.'

I want to visit you again. I don't want your possessions, I want you. I will gladly give all that I have and all that I am for you.

Will I still find you arguing? During my last visit I warned that I would punish those who continue to sin, because Christ speaks through me and he is not weak in dealing with you. I write strongly so that I won't have to make harsh use of God's authority when I am with you.

The God of love and peace be with you.

Through God's grace, the people of Corinth returned to Christ. There were now flourishing Christian communities all the way from Jerusalem around the inland sea and throughout Macedonia.

I decided to embark on a journey I had often longed to make. I wanted to preach about Jesus in Spain – and beyond. I would travel via Rome, the capital of the Roman Empire. There were already strong Christian communities in Rome – the news had spread there by others doing God's work – but they were heavily persecuted and needed encouragement.

Before I could set sail, I had to deliver the collection from Corinth to the churches in Jerusalem. I wrote to the Roman church about my plans.

Grace and peace to God's people in Rome.

I pray that I can visit you soon. God will reward with eternal life people who continue to do good. He will be angry with those who do evil. Jesus's death and resurrection reveal God's faith from the beginning to the end. Having heard the good news, you have no excuse for wickedness.

Do not judge others. Only God can judge. He will judge each of us, whether Jew or Gentile, because he loves us equally. The Torah is not important; we can sin and perish with or without the law. The real value in being a Jew is the knowledge that Jews were entrusted with the word of God. Righteousness through faith in Christ is there for all who believe.

As Christians we endure great suffering, but this develops our perseverance, character and hope. Our present suffering is nothing compared with the glory to come.

Through Jesus's death we have died to the power of sin; it has no power over us because we are alive to God in Jesus Christ. Offer yourselves in service, as living sacrifices to God. This will lead to holiness and eternal life, whereas sin leads to death. The Torah is not sin, but it preoccupies us with sin whilst Christ Jesus calls us to be concerned with goodness. None of us is perfect because even our best efforts go wrong, but if the Holy Spirit works in us our spirit is alive with goodness.

God works for the good of those who love him. Nothing can separate us from the love of God that is in Christ Jesus. If you proclaim that Jesus is Lord and believe in your heart that God raised him from the dead, you will be saved.

Use your gifts to help each other, not to impress the world. Be sincere. Hate evil and cling to good. Honour others above yourselves. Be joyful in hope, patient in suffering, faithful in prayer. Share with those in need, and offer hospitality. Rejoice with those who rejoice; mourn with those who mourn. Bless those who persecute you, and feed your enemy if he is hungry. Overcome evil with good. Work towards peace.

Love your neighbour as yourself, and stop passing judgement on each other. The strong among you must bear with the failings of the weak; you must accept one another just as Christ accepts you.

I am convinced that you are full of goodness. I will visit you on my way to Spain, but first I must go to Jerusalem, even though I have been warned against it. Pray for me. Glory to God forever.

Unfortunately things didn't go according to plan – God's plans were quite different. It was to be three long years before I finally arrived in Rome, and then as a prisoner.

From Corinth I took the collection to Jerusalem, where it came as no surprise to find myself at the centre of a riot when I visited the temple. Fortunately I am a Roman citizen as well as a Jew and a Christian, so Roman soldiers saved me from the bloodthirsty crowd by arresting me.

My friends and I, including Timothy, were taken to Caesarea, where the Romans kept us for two years before deciding to take us to Rome. At last we were going to Rome, even if it wasn't in the way we had intended. But God had yet another surprise for me.

It was early autumn, a dangerous time of year to sail on the Mediterranean. In a violent

storm we were shipwrecked on the shore of
Malta. By God's grace, everybody from the ship
survived. God had given me this unexpected
opportunity to introduce the good news about
Jesus to Malta. It was three months before we
had a ship to continue our journey. Eventually
we reached mainland Italy, and walked the rest
of the way to Rome.

My imprisonment until now has been light. I have been allowed to receive visitors and even to talk to people about Jesus. It is only recently, since I was formally charged, that they have stopped these favours and stopped me sending letters. Before that, I managed to write to the church in Philippi.

From Paul and Timothy to all Christ's saints in Philippi.

My shipwreck in Malta and imprisonment in Rome have helped to advance the good news. My guards see how I bear my chains for Christ, and Christians in Rome now speak more fearlessly. I rejoice because I know that through your prayers and the spirit of Jesus Christ I will be delivered – somehow. I don't know whether I am to live or to die. It would be better to die and to be with Christ, but as it is more important to continue my work, I trust they will spare me.

Don't be frightened of those who oppose you. Your courage will show them that they will be destroyed and you will be saved by Christ. Christ gives us encouragement, comfort and compassion. Like him, we should be servants to others and do everything with humility. In this dark world you will shine like stars.

I want to know Christ and to share in his suffering so that I too may have eternal life. I am imperfect, but God has called me. The destiny of Christ's enemies is destruction, but we await the Lord who will save us. Stand firm. Concentrate on all that is true, noble, pure and admirable. The peace of God which is beyond all understanding will guard your hearts and minds.

Thank you for your concern for me. Don't worry – I have strength for anything through Jesus Christ. You have sent generous gifts which I welcome; they are pleasing to God, and he will reward you with his glorious riches in Christ Jesus.

I hope to send Timothy to you soon. I will follow.

The grace of our Lord Jesus Christ be with you.

That was one of the last letters I sent. My situation is now serious by the ways of the world, but I'm not afraid of death. I have my faith to strengthen me. I constantly rejoice in my blessings from the Lord.

They have charged me with challenging Roman authority by preaching that Christ is the one true Lord, but as I have taught people to respect Roman authority they won't be able to prove this case against me.

The second charge, however, is more justified. I refuse to worship the Emperor as a god because there is only one true God. Should it be my fate to die, I look forward to meeting Christ in person, but I believe that I will be freed. I am sure God has more work for me to do.

I thank God that I have had time to complete this account. May you who read it live in the love of Jesus Christ.

Rome

ITALY

SPAIN

MALTA

MACEDONIA

Philippi
Thessalonica
THESSAL

GREECE
Corinth

MEDITERRANEAN

PAUL'S TRAVELS

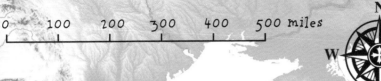

N
W E
S

0   100   200   300   400   500 miles

BLACK SEA

GALATIA

IA

ASIA MINOR

Ephesus •

• Lystra

• Tarsus

Antioch •

SYRIA

CYPRUS

SEA

Damascus •

Caesarea Philippi •

PALESTINE

Jerusalem •

JUDEA

ARABIA

TAKING THINGS FURTHER
The real read

This *Real Reads* volume of *Paul of Tarsus* is our interpretation of some of the events of the New Testament, told from the perspective of one of its most influential participants. In writing this account of Paul's life, we have used evidence from both The Acts of the Apostles and from some of Paul's letters, known as epistles, found in later books of the New Testament.

It is important to acknowledge that Acts of the Apostles and Paul's epistles are often contradictory. When difficulties arose, we tried to use evidence from the epistles rather than from Acts, as they are Paul's actual words. There is, however, uncertainty about which epistles were genuinely written by Paul. We have used those most commonly accepted as 'Pauline' epistles – Romans 1 and 2, Corinthians, Galatians, Philippians and Thessalonians 1. Philemon is also recognised as Paul's work, but was not necessary for our story.

At first, inconsistencies made our task rather difficult, until we realised that what we needed to do was present the New Testament as it is, rather than weave a path of our choice. Therefore, if you read *Real Reads Simon Peter*, for which we used Acts as a source, and *Real Reads Paul of Tarsus*, you may well notice some of the apparent contradictions and inconsistencies that are present in the Bible itself.

Although Paul's own writings provide us with a wealth of evidence to draw upon, we have also had to fill in some gaps by trying to imagine what he might have been like and what he might have thought. We have always based our work on thorough research and close attention to the Bible account.

This *Real Reads Paul of Tarsus* does not cover all the events of the New Testament. Reading the other five books in the series will bring you closer to an understanding of the complete story. You may then want to read the New Testament itself. We recommend that you read either the *New International Version* or *The Youth Bible*, details of which are given below.

Biblical sources

On the *Real Reads* website you will find an online concordance (www.realreads.co.uk/ newtestament/concordance/paul). A 'bible concordance' is an indexing tool which allows you to see how the same words, sentences and passages appear in different versions and translations of the Bible. This online concordance will direct you from events in the *Real Reads* version back to their biblical sources, so you can see clearly where each part of our story is drawn from.

Life in New Testament times

Paul was brought up as a Jew in Tarsus, in what is now southern Turkey. Tarsus is a long way from Palestine, so influences upon the young Paul would have been quite different from the childhood experiences of Jesus and his friends. Jews in Tarsus were a minority, meaning that Paul lived among Gentiles. He would probably have spoken at least two languages and, as Tarsus was known as an intellectual centre, he could have received a thorough classical education.

Tarsus, like Judea, was within the Roman Empire. At the time, the Romans ruled most of the land bordering the Mediterranean. In order to move around their enormous empire, the Romans built an impressive transport network, which helped to make Paul's travels much easier than they would otherwise have been. Over a period of thirty years, Paul travelled about ten thousand miles.

Paul visited many of the major cities of the time. Although these would have looked impressive, many of their inhabitants lived in great poverty. These people needed something to give them hope and purpose. The word 'gospel' means good news – Paul brought them good news about how they could live, and taught that Jesus's death gave everybody the chance of eternal happiness after a life of goodness. Paul believed that this message was for everybody, not only for Jews.

Within the Roman Empire people worshipped many different gods. Paul's message – as had been the message of all Jews for the past two thousand years – was that there was only one true god.

Unfortunately for Paul, many Jews saw all teaching about Jesus as a threat to their own religion. Romans too saw the new Christian movement as a problem – not least because they insisted that the Emperor was a god. As a result, Christians were heavily persecuted by both Jews and Romans. The beginnings of the early church were therefore far from easy or peaceful. The early Christians were courageous people, so convinced of the truth of Jesus that they were prepared to die for it. Paul himself suffered many severe beatings and imprisonment, and it is commonly believed that he eventually died for his Christian beliefs.

Paul's life and teaching have shaped Christianity into the faith it is today. By preaching to Gentiles he transformed what was a small Jewish sect into the beginnings of a world religion which would long outlast the Roman Empire.

Finding out more

We recommend the following books and websites to gain a greater understanding of Paul and his role in the New Testament.

Books

We strongly recommend that you read the rest of the *Real Reads* New Testament series, as the six narratives interlock to give a more complete picture of events. These are *Jesus of Nazareth, Mary of Galilee, Simon Peter, Judas Iscariot* and *Mary Magdalene.*

- *New Century Youth Bible*, Authentic Lifestyle, 2007.

- *Paul's Travels*, Tim Dowley, Candle Books, 2009.

- *Paul: A Novel*, Walter Wangerin, Lion Hudson, 2001.

- *In the Steps of Saint Paul: An Illustrated Guide to Paul's Journeys*, Peter Walker, Lion Hudson, 2008.

Websites

- www.apostlepaulthefilm.com/paul
Includes an interactive timeline in which Paul's life is shown alongside historical events, and animated maps of his journeys.

- www.gardenofpraise.com/bibleles.htm#paul
Lots of information, ideas and activities.

- www.ccel.org/bible/phillips/
CN600NTWORLD.htm
Short articles about the Roman Empire in New Testament times, accompanied by maps.

TV and film

- *Saul of Tarsus* and *The Ministry of Paul*, two titles from *Animated Stories from the New Testament*, directed by Richard Rich, Boulevard Entertainment, 1990.

- *Apostle Paul and the Earliest Churches*, Vision Video, 2005. A 50-minute documentary about Paul's ministry in what is now Turkey.

Food for thought

Here are some things to think about if you are reading *Paul of Tarsus* alone, and ideas for discussion if you are reading it with friends.

Starting points

- What kind of man do you think Paul was? What do you admire in his character? Is there anything you dislike?

- What reasons does Paul give for his early determination to stop the followers of Jesus?

- How do you think Paul felt when he realised that he was wrong, and was forced to change his opinions entirely?

- Can you explain the difference of opinion between Paul and the members of the early church in Jerusalem?

- If you were Simon Peter and you had known Jesus very well, what might you think about Paul? Why?

- What influence do you think Paul's teachings have upon Christians today?

Group activities

- Can you remember a time when you had to change your mind about something very important after learning something new? Talk about any such experience with the group. How easy was it to admit that you might have been wrong?

- Read Paul's account of his conversion and his baptism by Ananias, and act out the events. Interview Paul and Ananias about their feelings.

- Imagine you are the recipients of one of Paul's letters. Discuss together how you feel upon receiving the letter. What might you decide to do about it?

- If you have all read the other five books in this *Real Reads* New Testament series, discuss which people you think have had the greatest influence upon the Christian faith today. Which person did you find the most interesting, and why?

MARY MAGDALENE

www.realreads.co.uk

Retold by Alan Moore and Gill Tavner
Illustrated by Karen Donnelly

Published by Real Reads Ltd
Stroud, Gloucestershire, UK
www.realreads.co.uk

First published in 2010

ISBN 978-1-906230-27-2

Printed in China by Imago Ltd
Designed by Lucy Guenot
Typeset by Bookcraft Ltd, Stroud, Gloucestershire

CONTENTS

THE CHARACTERS

Mary Magdalene

Jesus brings light into Mary's dark life. How can she help him? What important role will she play?

Sarah

Anxious to help Mary, Sarah invites her to listen to a visiting preacher. Little does she know where this will lead.

Jesus

Jesus wants to show everybody the light that Mary has seen. Why do they find it so difficult to believe him?

Simon Peter

Simon Peter is a true and trusted friend of Jesus. How will he respond to Mary Magdalene when she joins the group?

Judas

Judas is in charge of the disciples' money. How will this affect his relationship with Mary Magdalene?

Pharisees

Insisting upon the Jewish law, these men find Jesus a difficult man to understand.

John

John is one of Jesus's disciples. What important responsibility will he be given?

MARY MAGDALENE

I wonder what people will say about me in the future. Will they be able to accept that a woman could be a devoted follower of God's son? Will they accept the nature of my love for Jesus?

When he was alive, I would have died for him. Now, a year after his death, I have devoted my life to spreading his word. Yes – at this point in history I am free to play this role. I wonder how history will view this time. How will it view me?

I grew up in Magdala, on the western shore of the Sea of Galilee. My parents, devout Jews, were gentle and loving. They taught me the scriptures and Jewish laws. All in all, the first twelve years of my life were very happy years, unspoilt by any foreboding of what lay ahead.

My happiness ended not long after my twelfth birthday. My father died of a sudden illness, leaving me and my mother heartbroken. In spite of her grief, mother had to take care of me. Having no money of her own, she had to remarry. My new stepfather was an angry and violent man who treated me and my mother terribly. I feared and hated him.

However, mother had achieved her goal. He was a wealthy man whose eventual death when I was twenty-two left us financially independent.

But what good is money when your mind and soul are damaged? That was me throughout my twenties. I was prone to regular deep depressions in which my mind spiralled uncontrollably downwards. In those periods, nothing could lift me. The future seemed dark, very dark.

I was terrified of men. I tried to avoid company whenever possible, preferring to be alone in my darkness. I hated meeting strangers. I certainly didn't want to accept an invitation to a family wedding in Cana, but my mother insisted. 'You don't have to stay long, Mary. Just show your face. Please.'

Cana is a small town to the west of Magdala. I set off reluctantly, unaware that this was the beginning of a new life – a journey towards light.

After the ceremony, I found a seat in a corner of the feasting room from which I could watch the other guests without attracting any attention to myself. A group of men caught my notice, especially the one called Jesus, who appeared to be the group's leader. Jesus's mother was there too – I watched as he guided her gently into a seat near me. That was what most struck me the first time I saw Jesus – his gentleness.

Jesus and his friends seemed intense but cheerful. They entered into the spirit of the celebrations with great energy, especially one of them, a strong, enthusiastic man. It was he who served food and drink to the others. 'Hey, Simon, could you bring us more wine?' called one of his friends.

'No problem,' he smiled. Simon soon returned, carrying a jug, from which he first served Jesus's mother. She took a sip and leant towards her son. 'This is water. They must

have run out of wine,' I heard her say softly. 'The host will be terribly embarrassed. Can you help him?'

I watched with interest.

'Mother – why involve me?' responded Jesus. 'My time has not yet come.'

She smiled at him. Turning to one of the servants, she quietly advised, 'Do whatever my son tells you.' By now I was fascinated.

Jesus pointed to six large jars. 'Fill those with water,' he told the bemused servants. They did as he asked. 'Now draw some out and take it to the host of the banquet.' One of the servants presented the embarrassed host with a cup filled from one of the jars, pointing to Jesus as he did so.

As soon as the host drank from the cup, a look of wonder brightened his features. For a moment he was stupefied, then his servants swung into action. Soon every pitcher and jug available was being used to fill guests' cups with wine.

A merry guest called out to the host. 'Heh – you sly old thing!' he joked. 'You should have served this wine first. Why did you save the best till now?'

Jesus concentrated on his food, trying to avoid being noticed.

I puzzled for months over what had happened, but found no explanation. It was not until my mother persuaded me to return to Cana to visit the newlyweds that I came across Jesus again and began to understand.

I was in one of my dark periods. Mother thought the change of scene would help. I doubted it, but hadn't the energy to resist.

Fortunately, Sarah, the new wife, was kind and sensitive to my condition, offering me both friendship and space. On my second day there, she suggested gently, 'It might do you good to come out with me this afternoon. A man from Nazareth is preaching in town. He's supposed to be a fantastic speaker.'

'I'm not sure,' I hesitated. 'I don't like crowds.'

'Oh, come on,' she insisted. 'It might be our only chance to hear Jesus.'

'Did you say Jesus?'

Sarah nodded. 'Yes. He was at our wedding.'

It was easy to find Jesus; we just followed
the crowd. Sarah had to lead me by the hand as
I was afraid to raise my eyes from the ground.
I was afraid of people's faces. Panic rose within
me as I saw more and more feet, all stirring
the dust.

'There he is!' exclaimed Sarah. I couldn't
look. I was dizzy, struggling for breath. I pulled
against Sarah. 'This way.' Sarah guided me to
the side of a house, away from the crowd. We
went through the cooler air of the house to the
courtyard, where we stood in the doorway just
behind Jesus. Here I could breathe more easily.

I recognised Jesus immediately. We were so
close that we could almost touch him. Jesus's
attention was fixed upon an important-looking
man who knelt at his feet. Sarah whispered
to me that he was a royal official from
Capernaum. 'My son is dying,' he told Jesus.

'Please, come with me to Capernaum. Save him.'

The crowd looked eager. What was Jesus
going to do? I wondered whether they would
follow him all the way to Capernaum. Jesus
looked up from the man with a sigh, and spoke
to the people before him. 'You want to see a
miracle to prove who I am. Why do you need to
see a sign before you believe?'

I wondered what on earth he meant, but the
official was more intent on saving his son than
in asking questions.

'Please help my child,' he begged.

'Your son lives,' Jesus assured him.

'But won't you come to him?'

'Your son lives,' repeated Jesus.

We learned later that the man's son had recovered at the exact time that Jesus had said those words. The official became a follower of Jesus. I suppose that proved Jesus's point. Would I ever have believed that Jesus was the Son of God without the evidence in Cana, or without what happened to me later that very evening? I don't know.

Two of Sarah's friends invited Jesus to stay in their home. They suggested that Sarah and I dine with them. I was reluctant to accept, but Sarah was keen and I didn't want to disappoint her.

That evening, although I tried to make myself invisible in the shadows, I found myself fascinated by Jesus. Something drew me to him, a force I had never experienced before. I couldn't take my eyes off him, even when he looked in my direction, even when he walked towards me. He sat down beside me, and still I stared. He took my hands in his. 'Mary, you are troubled,' he said gently.

The rest of the room grew silent – or perhaps I just stopped noticing their noise. Jesus seemed aware only of me; nothing else. I started to cry, but I didn't feel embarrassed. Jesus's gaze never left my face; his gentle hands simply held mine tighter.

'Your troubles are in the past,' he whispered. 'Hear my word and believe. I will give you new life.'

Something in the way that he looked at me, giving me his full attention without seeking anything from me, convinced me. My darkness lifted, never to return. This man was truly the light of the world.

'Mary, you seem different,' observed Sarah as we walked home.

'I've changed,' I said, though I wasn't really sure exactly what I meant.

'Mary, you seem different,' observed my mother upon my return to Magdala. I told her everything that had happened. 'I'd like to meet Jesus again,' I concluded, 'but I'm not sure how.'

'You'll find him,' my mother assured me. 'He'll probably be in Jerusalem for the Passover.'

Like most Jews, we always went to Jerusalem to celebrate the Passover. Everyone looked forward to it, and this year, for the first time in many years, so did I.

I wondered how I would possibly find Jesus amongst so many people, but it wasn't difficult. I knew that he now had many followers, so I found a crowd and there he was. Noticing me immediately, he made space for me beside him. 'How are you, Mary?' he asked. He remembered me!

As we walked at the head of the crowd, Jesus explained his mission to create heaven on earth by demonstrating God's love, and clear the way for us all to reach God. I decided that – as much as was possible for a woman – I would follow him and support his work. But I didn't really know how I could do that. What could I offer?

The next morning was the Sabbath. I accompanied Jesus to a pool at Bethesda. Many sick and disabled people visit this pool, hoping to be healed by its waters. Jesus knelt beside a

sorrowful elderly man lying on a mat at the water's edge. 'I have been visiting this pool for thirty-eight years,' explained the man, 'but nobody helps me into the water.'

'If you want to get well,' Jesus told him, 'why don't you pick up your mat and walk?' I watched as the man did just that. 'Now,' said Jesus quite sternly, 'give up your sinful ways, or worse will happen.'

Puzzled by his comment, I asked Jesus what he meant. 'This man's biggest problem isn't his illness. Like all human beings his relationship with God is broken. That is what I have come to mend.'

As I watched the healed man pick his way through the other sick people, I wondered how such brokenness could be fixed. I decided to give everything I had to help Jesus.

I joined Jesus and his followers as often as I could. Some of my friends were scandalised that I travelled with a group of men, but I didn't care what they thought.

My mother understood. We talked for hours about Jesus. I think she was so pleased that my depression had gone, and that the

scars left by my
stepfather had healed,
that she would have
given anything to
Jesus in gratitude. 'Use
our money to support his
mission,' she told me.

At first some of Jesus's
friends seemed a little uncomfortable
with my presence but, following his example,
they gradually accepted me. Simon was perhaps
the most welcoming, whilst Judas, in charge of
the group's funds, appreciated the important
contribution I could make. He seemed pleased, in
spite of himself, when some of my wealthy friends
also joined us.

On one occasion Simon took us across the Sea
of Galilee in his boat, to where a great crowd waited
on the opposite shore. Jesus led everybody onto a
hillside and began to preach. I watched in wonder
as the crowd continued to grow. By the time dusk

gathered, there must have been around five thousand people. Five thousand hungry people, I thought to myself.

Judas must have been thinking the same thing. 'Shall we go into the town to buy food?' he suggested, looking to me for support.

'No, we'll feed them now,' replied Jesus. He took what little food we had – five barley loaves and two fish. He gave thanks to God, broke it into pieces, and told us to distribute it among the people. Tentatively, we picked up the baskets he gave us and began to distribute the crumbs. I was 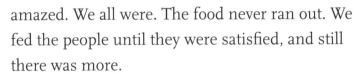 amazed. We all were. The food never ran out. We fed the people until they were satisfied, and still there was more.

That evening Jesus prayed alone, leaving the crowd to wonder at what had happened.

Jesus was often frustrated by people's desperation to see signs and miracles. 'Why?' he once asked me. 'Why do their eyes need to see before their hearts can believe?' But he knew that he had to keep providing signs – even to his closest friends.

After feeding the crowd, Jesus stayed late in the mountains. Simon offered to sail the rest of us back across the water to Capernaum. Thanks to our many trips to and fro over Galilee I was becoming used to sailing, but I can't say I ever felt confident in a boat. That night, the stormy weather and choppy water awakened my old fears. Simon offered to keep watch while we all slept, but I couldn't sleep. 'Don't worry. We'll be fine,' Simon assured me.

Suddenly I spotted something moving towards us over the water, though my eyes were partially blinded by the sea-spray. 'Simon! What's that?' I whispered.

'I don't know,' admitted Simon, wiping water from his own eyes. I was now gripping Simon's arm. Together, we peered into the darkness.

'Don't be afraid.' We heard the familiar voice at the same time as Jesus's features became clear. He walked across the water to us and climbed into the boat. 'Why did you doubt?' he asked calmly.

25

Some of the crowd left behind on the shore soon found boats to follow us. When they found Jesus already in Capernaum they were puzzled. 'Rabbi, how did you get here?' they asked.

Jesus replied, 'Admit it. You are looking for me because I fed you when you were hungry.' They nodded. 'Believe with your hearts instead of your stomachs. Food rots. Search instead for food that lasts for ever – search for bread for your soul.'

'How can we find such bread?' they asked.

'I bring it from God. This is what I am. Believe in me, the one God has sent.'

'Show us a miracle to help us believe. Do something like Moses did when he fed his people manna in the desert.'

Hadn't Jesus just done exactly that? Why did they keep demanding signs? Why seek answers to their smaller problems rather than their biggest one?

Nevertheless, Jesus replied calmly. 'The

manna that Moses fed his people was just bread. The bread of life is the one that gives life to the world.' People seemed puzzled. Jesus had to spell it out more clearly. 'I am the bread of life. He who comes to me will never go hungry.' Most people still seemed perplexed.

'My friends – you have seen me, and still you doubt! Listen, I have come down from heaven to do my father's will. I am the bread from heaven that you may eat and never die.'

Some people fell to their knees in prayer, but I heard others muttering 'blasphemy'. In spite of hearing Jesus's words and seeing his work, they were still not convinced. One man called out, 'Are you saying you are equal to God?'

Such accusations could result in a person being stoned to death. A shiver ran down my spine. For the first time I felt concerned for Jesus's safety.

I returned home to visit my mother and to replenish my funds, agreeing to meet Jesus and the disciples in Jerusalem a few weeks later. When I returned I brought with me some friends – other women of independent wealth who were keen to support Jesus's work.

We met Jesus in the women's court of the temple. Within minutes, our attention was drawn to something happening in the entrance. We watched as a group of men dragged a distressed woman roughly over the dusty ground. They dropped her at Jesus's feet, where she knelt, weeping. 'Teacher,' one man

explained breathlessly, 'this woman has been with a man other than her husband. Moses commanded us to stone such women. What shall we do?'

I sensed immediately that these men wanted to trap Jesus. If he said that the woman should be released, he would be defying Jewish law. On the other hand his whole message was one of forgiveness. He could not condemn this poor woman to a cruel death by stoning.

Squatting down, Jesus traced patterns in the dust with his finger. I think he was demonstrating his lack of interest in the men's accusations. When they pressed him again for an answer, he looked up at them. 'If any one of you is without sin, let him throw the first stone.' Then he returned his attention to the dust.

The men fell silent. They shuffled their feet uncomfortably. One by one, they drifted away, leaving the accused woman weeping on the ground. I helped her to her feet.

'Stand up,' said Jesus to the woman. 'Who now is here to condemn you?'

She looked around. 'Nobody, Master.'

'And I do not condemn you either. Go now, and sin no more.'

How could such a gentle man make so many enemies? I couldn't understand it, but I saw, with increasing fear, that it was true. I suppose Jesus spoke truths that people did not want to hear. These people didn't just reject his teaching – they really hated and feared him. I worried about him constantly.

Jesus's message was so simple, so peaceful. He said that we should love God and love each other. 'I am the light of the world,' he often said. 'Whoever follows me will no longer walk in darkness, but have eternal life.' He had certainly replaced my darkness with light, but I don't think he meant it literally. He meant that he brought us all a clear view of the way to God.

I particularly remember one occasion when Jesus outraged his opponents. During his teaching one day, he said, 'I bring the truth that will set you free.'

One of the religious leaders was furious. 'But Abraham, the father of the Jewish nation, freed our people from slavery centuries ago!' he sputtered. 'You can't set us free! We are not slaves!'

'You are slaves to your sins,' replied Jesus. 'How can you claim to be Abraham's children when you would kill me for speaking the truth? Abraham wouldn't have done that! You speak the words of the devil, and therefore you are children of the devil.'

I had never experienced such tension. I held my breath.

People's faces were red, their fists clenched. 'We are the children of God! You are the one possessed by the devil!'

'If you were God's children, you would love me and believe what I say.'

'Are you claiming to be greater than Abraham?' they asked.

Jesus looked at them and responded with staggering simplicity. 'Before Abraham was born, I am.' He walked away through the crowd.

I finally breathed again. I felt faint. Had Jesus *really* just told us that he was God, here among us?

Jesus's work never ceased. He still had to provide many signs before people would believe who he was. 'The poor people,' he once sighed when alone with me. 'They are so blind.'

One Sabbath I found Jesus and his disciples outside the temple. They were talking to a blind beggar. As I watched, Jesus gathered some dust and spat on it to make a little mud which he spread over the blind man's eyes. 'Go and wash your eyes in the Pool of Siloam,' he directed.

When the man had left, Jesus told us, 'As long as I am here I must do God's work. For this short time that I am in the world, I must help people to see.'

Later, Judas and I went to buy food for the others. 'I wonder what happened to that blind man?' mused Judas. He was soon answered when we noticed a small crowd, at the centre of which we saw the man talking with great excitement. 'Honestly!' he cried, 'When I washed the mud from my eyes at Siloam, I could see! I can see you all now – you, who know that I've been blind since birth!'

The amazed crowd didn't know how to act. 'We should take him to see the Pharisees,' they decided. 'They'll know what to do.'

'Let's follow,' Judas whispered to me.

The Pharisees looked distinctly uncomfortable when they heard the man's story. 'Jesus can't be from God,' they declared, after some thought, 'because he broke God's law by healing you on the Sabbath!'

'But he must be from God. How else could he make a blind man see?' responded one man in the crowd. He turned to the healed man. 'It was your eyes he opened. What do you say about him?'

'I was blind, but now I can see,' was his simple

reply. 'I've already told you what happened. How can you possibly doubt who Jesus is? He must be from God to have done this.'

His impatience enraged the Pharisees. 'This man is pretending. He must be working for Jesus.' They knew that they would have to discredit the man to stop the crowd believing him. 'You were blind from your birth,' they shouted. 'Blindness is a punishment for sin! How dare you, a sinner, lecture us?'

Judas drew the healed man away from the crowd. 'Come with us,' he said softly. 'We'll take you back to Jesus.'

Of course, Jesus welcomed him with open arms. 'Do you believe in the Son of God?' he asked.

'Who is he, Master? Tell me, so that I can believe in him.'

'You see me now before you,' replied Jesus. 'I have come into this world so that the blind will see.'

The man fell to his knees. 'Lord, I believe!'

Jesus truly loved everybody, even those who opposed him. He likened himself to a good shepherd. A good shepherd, he told us, would lay down his life for his flock. This filled me with dread. I had no doubt at all that Jesus would be prepared to lay down his life for his flock if he had to. His love for others was pure and selfless; it never failed him, whatever the test.

Of course, Jesus had some particularly close friends in addition to those of us who followed him. Whenever we were in Bethany, we visited the sisters Mary and Martha and their brother, Lazarus. I formed a close friendship with Martha. She was a very practical woman. One day Jesus heard from Martha that Lazarus was dangerously ill.

'We should go now,' I urged. 'Martha wouldn't trouble you unless she was really worried.'

'We'll complete our work here first,' Jesus replied.

My head told me that I had to trust Jesus, but the tightness in my stomach matched the fear I felt.

Two days later Jesus gathered us all together. 'Our friend Lazarus has died,' he told us. 'We must go to him.' How did he know?

By the time we reached Bethany, Lazarus had been dead for four days. Dressed in black, Martha emerged from her house. When she hugged me, I felt her trembling. She turned to Jesus, tears in her eyes. 'Lord, if you had come earlier Lazarus wouldn't have died.'

Jesus held her close to him. 'Martha, I am the resurrection and the life. Whoever believes in me will never die. Do you believe this?'

'Yes, Lord.'

'Lazarus will rise again.'

'I know that he'll rise to heaven, Lord, but we want him here with us.'

Her sister Mary emerged from the house and sank to her knees before Jesus. Her words echoed Martha's. 'Lord, if you had been here Lazarus would still be alive.'

Moved by their distress, Jesus asked them to lead us to Lazarus's tomb. When we arrived, Simon helped him to move aside the huge stone sealing the entrance. Jesus prayed. 'Father, thank you for hearing me. Let these people see and believe.' Then he called, 'Lazarus, come out!'

We held our breath and stared at the hole in the rock. There was a shuffling sound. A slight movement. I gasped as Lazarus walked from the tomb. His strong, healthy body was still wrapped in his burial shroud.

Not even death could defeat Jesus.

Bethany was close to Jerusalem, so Mary, Martha and Lazarus were able to update us with news from the city. The ever-increasing number of people believing that Jesus was the Son of God was making both the Romans and the Jewish leaders nervous. 'The Pharisees have asked the Sanhedrin to find a way to stop you,' Lazarus warned Jesus. The Sanhedrin was the governing council, and held a great deal of power. 'The high priest has said that it's better for one good man to die than for the whole Jewish nation to perish.'

'It's too soon,' said Jesus quietly. 'We will go away to the desert, to Ephraim. We'll come back in time for the Passover.'

'I'll stay here with our friends and await your return,' I said.

We knew that Jesus would keep his word. When the time came for his return, Martha and I prepared a special meal. Mary took all her savings and went to buy perfume to anoint Jesus. I understood her desire – her concerns were always more spiritual than those of her sister.

Crowds gathered outside the house. Word of Lazarus's resurrection had spread far and wide, and people were eager to see both men. That night, at dinner, Jesus warned Lazarus. 'The crowds bring danger. You should keep a low profile until I am gone.'

'Gone, Lord?' asked Mary. Then, weeping, she poured her expensive perfume over Jesus's feet.

Jesus noticed Judas's shocked expression. 'Judas, you think Mary should have given her money to the poor, don't you? The poor will always be amongst you, but you will not always have me. Mary's gift prepares me for my burial.'

The following day Jesus rode into Jerusalem.
Martha and I had gone ahead. As Jesus
approached we joined the crowds lining the
streets, waving palm branches and shouting.
Our scriptures had told us that our king would
enter Jerusalem on a donkey and that we

shouldn't be afraid. I tried not to think about what the scriptures said would happen next.

That night, Jesus invited his disciples to share their last meal together. It was traditional that only men should attend such meals, so I stayed with Mary and Martha. It wasn't until after Jesus's death that Simon told me about that night's terrible events.

'Jesus washed our feet!' exclaimed Simon. 'I objected, but he said I had to let him wash me or I was no part of him. He told us to serve others as he served us. After the meal,' continued Simon more quietly, 'he said that one of us would betray him.'

'I know,' I sighed sadly. 'The others told me when they returned to Bethany. They told me about everything Judas did.'

'How could he do it, Mary?' Simon broke down in tears. 'How could Judas betray Jesus?'

Simon fell silent. I placed my hand on his shoulder, but he shrugged it off. 'I don't deserve your sympathy, Mary. I too have betrayed Jesus.'

'Simon, surely you're the last person on earth who would ... '

'Oh, Mary!' he interrupted me. 'I followed when they arrested him. They took him to the high priest's house. I watched them whip him. I watched his skin being torn from his body.' Simon's hands covered his eyes, as though trying to shield them from the terrible things he had seen. 'Such pain!'

I tried to comfort him. 'You couldn't have helped.'

'It's worse that that, Mary. I was so scared.' He paused and took a deep, trembling breath before he continued. 'I denied him three times, Mary. That night I told three people that I didn't know Jesus.'

I put my arms around him as he sobbed. 'Jesus would understand,' I soothed. 'You were afraid for your life.'

'My life is now his,' he resolved. 'I'll devote my remaining years to him. I will die for him.'

'I'm sure you will,' I answered. That wasn't exactly what I meant to say.

None of us slept on the night of Jesus's arrest. Early the next morning, John set out to search for Jesus's mother. She would be in Jerusalem for the Passover, and would be in need of comfort. I decided to try to find Jesus.

Arriving in the city, I heard the news that Jesus was to be crucified that day. Crucifixion – an agonising death on a cross – was the most terrible death imaginable. My knees collapsed beneath me. Only my determination to find Jesus gave me strength.

To find Jesus I did as I had always done – I followed the crowds. Bent low under the immense weight of a beam of wood, Jesus was barely recognisable. His body was broken and bruised, with open lacerations and dried blood. Flies buzzed around him. Soldiers were forcing him to carry his own cross to Golgotha, the place of crucifixion. Shocked, I joined a group of women following him.

Progress was so slow. Jesus stumbled often, and I ached to help him. At one point I noticed John in the crowd at the side of the road. Next to him stood Jesus's mother. John supported her weight as she watched her son pass by.

How can I find words to describe Jesus's crucifixion? I can only tell what I saw. Soldiers had nailed a sign above his head, saying 'The King of the Jews'. They wanted to humiliate him. They had pushed a crown of thorns on his head, from which blood still ran down his face. At the foot of his cross, where I knelt with Mary and John, soldiers gambled for the clothes they had taken from him.

Jesus looked down at his mother and John. 'Mother, this is your son,' he said. 'John, this is your mother. Care for her.'

His suffering was long and terrible. Near the end Jesus said 'I am thirsty.' Soldiers soaked a sponge in wine vinegar and put it to his lips. I could tell that he was praying. His eyes were closed but his lips were moving. He opened his eyes for one last time to look upon the world he so loved. With his final breath, he said, 'It is finished.'

Towards dusk, soldiers broke the legs of those being crucified who were still alive, so they could not press down on their feet and would suffocate more quickly. As Jesus appeared to be dead already, they pushed a spear into his side to be sure. Blood and water ran out.

We wept as they brought Jesus's body down from his cross. Joseph of Arimathea, an influential Jew and a secret follower of Jesus, arranged for Jesus's body to be buried in his own tomb.

The next morning, after another sleepless night, I arose before daybreak and walked to the tomb. It had been cut out of the rock and, like Lazarus's tomb, it had a stone across the entrance. Or at least it should have had. I stopped and stared in disbelief. The stone had been rolled back. The tomb was open. Dreading the sight that would greet me, I crept towards the opening and peered in. It was empty!

I don't know how to describe my feelings at that moment. Horror? Relief? Excitement? I turned and ran to the house in which Simon and John were looking after Mary. 'Simon!' I hammered on the door. 'Simon!'

He appeared. He looked exhausted.

'They've taken his body out of the tomb! I don't know where they've put him!'

Simon and John ran. I followed. I found them talking excitedly outside the tomb. I looked inside again, more calmly this time. I noticed that the burial clothes were neatly folded.

'We need to tell the others,' said Simon.

'I'll stay here.' I felt unable to leave. In a dreamlike state, I felt compelled to look in the tomb again. This time, I saw two beings dressed in white – they must have been angels – seated where the body had been.

'Why are you crying?' one of them asked.

'They have taken my Lord away, and I don't know where they've put him.'

The angels' eyes focused upon something behind me. A shiver ran down my spine as I turned, afraid of what I might see.

My eyes were blurred with tears. That's my only excuse for failing to recognise him – I suppose it's a feeble one. I thought it was the gardener. 'Why are you crying?' he asked. 'Who are you looking for?'

'Sir,' I wept, 'please tell me where you've put him.'

'Mary,' answered the man. I knew that voice.

'Rabboni!' I cried, 'Teacher!'

I threw myself towards him, but he stepped back.

'Do not reach for me now, for I have not yet returned to the father,' he explained. 'Go and tell the others that I am returning to my father.'

That evening we gathered together in secret. As Jesus's friends, our lives were in danger. Only one of our close group was missing – Thomas. We were all concerned for his safety.

The fear and tension in the room suddenly eased into an unexpected sense of calm. Jesus appeared in our midst, just as he had appeared to me outside his tomb. 'Peace be with you,' he said gently. 'Understand this. I had to take on the world's sins and clear the way to God by dying and living again. Now, as the father sent me, I am sending you.' Then he breathed on us. 'Receive the Holy Spirit,' he explained. 'If you forgive anyone their sins, those sins are forgiven.' While we all considered the enormity of his words, he disappeared from our sight.

A knock on the door announced Thomas's arrival. When we told him that Jesus had been there he looked hurt. 'Why do you say this? Why are you lying to me?' No matter how much we protested, he would not be convinced. 'Unless I see the nail marks in his hands and put my fingers into his wounds,' he said, 'I will not believe it.'

A week later we had all gathered in the same room. This time, Thomas was with us. Once again, we felt Jesus's calming presence. Thomas was wide-eyed. Jesus walked towards him, holding out his wounded hands. 'Put your fingers in my wounds, Thomas. Put your

hand in my side. Never doubt again.'

Thomas did as Jesus had invited and fell to his knees. 'My Lord and my God!'

'Thomas,' said Jesus, laying a hand upon his shoulder. 'You believe because you have seen me. Blessed are those who believe without needing to see me.'

I remember again the question Jesus once asked me. 'Why do people need to see before they can believe?'

We have all seen. Whether or not we would have believed without seeing is a question we often discuss, a question none of us can answer.

One thing, however, is certain. We are the lucky few. Our work now is to tell our story, so that other people might hear about Jesus. It will be more difficult for them, for you. We have to tell it in such a way that people will be able to believe without having to see.

This is how I will spend the rest of my life.

TAKING THINGS FURTHER
The real read

This *Real Reads* volume of *Mary Magdalene* is our interpretation of the events of the New Testament, told from the perspective of one of its most enigmatic and, recently, controversial participants. In writing this account of Mary Magdalene's life, we have used evidence from the gospel according to John. This is one of the four gospels – the first four books of the New Testament.

It is important to acknowledge that all four gospels were written after Jesus's death, and that the writers had different aims in mind – although they all wanted to engender faith in the reader that Jesus was the Son of God. The first three gospels – Matthew, Mark and Luke – are called 'the synoptic gospels'. They were probably written between forty and sixty years after the crucifixion. The gospel according to John, written later, is significantly different.

Sometimes, the four gospels' accounts of events differ considerably. At first this made our task rather difficult, until we realised that what we needed to do was present the New Testament as it is, rather than to weave a path of our choice between the gospels. Therefore, if you read all six books in the *Real Reads* New Testament series, you may well notice some of the apparent contradictions and inconsistencies that are present in the Bible itself.

In writing each of the six *Real Reads* New Testament books we chose a specific source to follow. To write Mary's account of her life we decided to use John's gospel, because it provides the most information about Mary. However, even in this gospel there is not a great deal of information. For *Mary Magdalene*, perhaps more than any of the other books in this series, we have had to add material from our own imaginations. Nevertheless, we have tried very hard to stay close to the New Testament evidence.

This *Real Reads Mary Magdalene* does not cover all the events of the New Testament.

Reading the other five books in the series will bring you closer to an understanding of the complete story. You may then want to read the New Testament itself. We recommend that you read either the *New International Version* or *The Youth Bible*, details of which are given below.

Biblical sources

Although *Mary Magdalene* is based on the story as told in the gospel of John, there are a few places where we have drawn on other sources.

On the *Real Reads* website you will find an online concordance (www.realreads.co.uk/ newtestament/concordance/marymagdalene). A 'bible concordance' is an indexing tool which allows you to see how the same words, sentences and passages appear in different versions and translations of the Bible. This online concordance will direct you from events in the *Real Reads* version back to their biblical sources, so you can see clearly where each part of our story is drawn from.

Life in
New Testament times

The main events of Mary Magdalene's life took place in Palestine, a long narrow area of land bordered to the west by the Mediterranean Sea and to the east by the Transjordanian Desert. Some parts of Palestine were desert, some were hill country, some rich pasture land, and some uncultivated wilderness. Mary was probably born in Magdala, on the western shore of Lake Galilee, an area with a mixed population of Jews and Gentiles, and a reputation for political unrest. She was probably from a wealthy family and she had wealthy friends.

Although Palestine was Jewish land, it was part of the Roman Empire and under Roman control. The Jews resented paying taxes to Rome. During Jesus's lifetime, there was considerable conflict between the Jews and their Roman rulers. This helps to explain why the Romans might have been nervous of the crowds following Jesus. It also helps to explain

N
W E
S

Capernaum
Cana   Magdala
GALILEE   SEA
                          OF
                        GALILEE
Nazareth

PALESTINE

RIVER JORDAN

Ephraim

Jerusalem

Bethany

0   10   20 miles

DEAD
SEA

why Mary often felt nervous about Jesus's safety.

You may notice that more women appear in *Real Reads Mary Magdalene* than in the other books in the series. These days, we assume that women played a very minor role in political life during Jesus's times, but that is not necessarily true. Many people accept that, over the centuries, women's roles in the story of Jesus have been significantly reduced. Mary could very well have been a leading member of the early church.

A great many things have been written about Mary Magdalene, and you may find it rewarding to research them further. You can decide for yourself which theory is most likely to be true.

Finding out more

We recommend the following books and websites to gain a greater understanding of the New Testament.

Books

We strongly recommend that you read the rest of the *Real Reads* New Testament series, as the six narratives interlock to give a more complete picture of events. These are *Jesus of Nazareth*, *Mary of Galilee*, *Simon Peter*, *Judas Iscariot*, and *Paul of Tarsus*.

- *New Century Youth Bible*, Authentic Lifestyle, 2007.

- *People in the Life of Jesus*, Colin Lumsden, Day One Publications, 2003. A colouring book.

- Sara Hartman, *Mary Magdalene's Easter Story*, Concordia, 2005.

- Mildred Tuck, *A Child's Book of Miracles and Wonders*, Standard Publishing, 2003.

Websites

- www.bbc.co.uk/religion/religions/christianity/history/marymagdalene.shtml
Lots of information about Mary Magdalene.

- www.magdalene.org
A useful site – targeted at adults, but with a short introduction to Mary Magdalene and some helpful links.

TV and film

- *Jesus of Nazareth*, directed by Franco Zeffirelli, ITV DVD, 1977. A six and a half hour mini-series.

- *The Miracles of Jesus*, Boulevard Entertainment, 2006. A short animated film.

- *Jesus Christ Superstar*, directed by Norman Jewison, Universal Pictures UK, 2005. This screen version of the 1970s rock opera by Tim Rice and Andrew Lloyd Webber focuses on Jesus's final days, but pays more attention to his relationship with Judas than to his relationship with Mary Magdalene.

Food for thought

Here are some things to think about if you are reading *Mary Magdalene* alone, and ideas for discussion if you are reading it with friends.

Starting points

- How many references can you find to darkness and light? Why do you think Mary calls Jesus 'the light of the world'?

- How does Mary decide to help Jesus? How important do you think this is?

- Make a list of the miracles Mary witnesses. What do you think a miracle is, and why do you think some people need to see them?

- Why do you think Jesus is saddened by people's need to experience miracles?

- Choose one of the miracles described in the book, and retell the story through the eyes of the person Jesus helped.

- Jesus describes himself in several ways – the good shepherd, the bread of life, and the light of the world. Choose one of these, and try to explain what you think he means.

- Many people have suggested that Mary and Jesus were married. If that had been true, how much do you think it would have changed the story?

- Mary is the first person to see the risen Christ. Some people think this makes her the first Christian. What do you think?

Group activities

- Together, make a list of all the references to women in this book. What roles do the different women play? How are they treated?

- With one person as a reporter, the others in the group can play the roles of the disciples, including Simon Peter and Judas. The reporter asks the disciples what they thought about Mary joining the group. Did their feelings change as time went on?

- Talk in the group about miracles. Do you believe in them? Do you think there are miracles in everyday life today?

- At the end of her story, Mary wonders whether she would have believed what had happened without seeing it for herself. Christians all over the world today believe the story without seeing it. Discuss with your group whether it is easy to believe things without having first-hand proof. Create a list of things you all believe without actually seeing any evidence – if there are any!

JUDAS
ISCARIOT

www.realreads.co.uk

Retold by Alan Moore and Gill Tavner
Illustrated by Karen Donnelly

Published by Real Reads Ltd
Stroud, Gloucestershire, UK
www.realreads.co.uk

First published in 2010

ISBN 978-1-906230-28-9

Printed in China by Imago Ltd
Designed by Lucy Guenot
Typeset by Bookcraft Ltd, Stroud, Gloucestershire

CONTENTS

THE CHARACTERS

Judas

For the first time in his life, Judas has a sense of purpose. Will Jesus live up to Judas's expectations?

Jesus

What is Jesus trying to achieve? Will he fulfil Judas's hopes? Does he already know where this friendship will lead?

Simon Peter

Simon Peter is one of Jesus's most trusted disciples. Can such different men as Simon and Judas work well together?

4

Pharisees

Pharisees are men of God and men of the law. Why might they see Jesus as a threat? Why does Judas want to confront them?

Levi

Levi is a tax collector, hated by the people. What point is Jesus making when he befriends him?

Zacharias

A Jewish priest and a friend of Judas's father, can Zacharias persuade Judas to help him? What does he hope to achieve?

Pontius Pilate

The Roman governor of the province. Will his decision save Judas from the consequences of his own actions?

JUDAS
ISCARIOT

Jesus smiled as his mother entertained us with stories about his childhood. 'He was only twelve,' she reminisced, 'but all the men on the temple steps were listening to him. He'd drawn quite a crowd.'

'No,' I gasped involuntarily. Everybody turned to me.

'Are you all right, Judas?' asked Andrew.

'Fine, thanks,' I said, but in truth I was rather shaken. Mary had awakened a long-dormant memory. Twenty years ago, still a boy myself, I had been in that crowd. I had seen Jesus talking to those men on the temple steps.

Like many Jewish boys, I accompanied my father to Jerusalem once a year to take part in the Passover festival, commemorating our people's freedom from slavery in Egypt. That particular year, my father had joined the other priests in the temple, leaving me alone and awkward on the steps.

Another boy was there, about my age. Like me, he was alone. I smiled, unsure what to say. He returned my smile, then turned away to join a group of men. Feeling rather rejected, I watched him. He spoke confidently, and the men listened intently. Why couldn't I be confident like him? The disappointment, longing and jealousy were too painful. I turned my back on him and crept into the temple.

Now, listening to Mary's memories of her son's childhood, I realised that the other boy on the temple steps all those years ago was Jesus himself.

That was when the end of my story was written.

Everyone expected me to follow in my father's footsteps and become a priest, but I was undecided. I felt uncomfortable with some aspects of Jewish law, or at least the way most priests interpreted it. Even in my twenties I was still uncertain. Then one day I met a man who gave me a new sense of purpose. At last I had a direction.

One spring I had accompanied my elderly father on a journey north to visit some relatives. On the way back we planned to rest in Capernaum on the shores of Lake Galilee. Wearily approaching the town, we noticed a crowd gathered on a dusty hillside. As we drew nearer, we could hear a man talking to them.

'Who is that?' I asked one of the listeners.

'Jesus of Nazareth,' he whispered.

Jesus of Nazareth! So this was the man everyone was talking about. I persuaded my father to stay and listen, eagerly pulling him into the crowd.

Jesus's words startled me, made my heart beat faster. Problems which had tormented me for years suddenly seemed simple. No priest had ever made such sense. I felt tears in my eyes. Embarrassed, I wiped them away. I felt I had been searching for this man all my life.

A few months earlier I had visited John the Baptist, a holy man who was calling on people to love God and to keep the laws given to us by Moses. I had thought he might be the one who would deliver our people from the Romans, refresh our laws, and make us a strong and God-fearing nation again.

John himself had made it clear that I was expecting too much of him. 'I am just a voice in the desert,' he told me, 'here to prepare the way for someone greater. When he comes he will baptise you with the Holy Spirit.'

Could Jesus be the man promised by John? Whether he was or not, I wanted to hear more. For the first time in my life I felt certain about something. I needed to follow Jesus.

My father tugged at my sleeve, his frail voice anxious. 'Come away, Judas. This man and his ideas will divide our people. He will only cause trouble.'

I looked at my father. I thought about his insistence on ritual and sacrifice; I thought about the wealth of the synagogues in such a poor land. 'I'm sorry, father,' I whispered, 'but I must go to him. I have no choice.'

Weeping, I turned away from my father and walked towards Jesus. The crowds were already dispersing. Unable to find the right words, I smiled at him.

Jesus seemed to have been expecting me. 'Follow me,' he said.

I did. It might have seemed a simple choice at the time, but – unfortunately for me – nothing is ever simple.

I soon settled into Jesus's group. Some of the men lived in Capernaum, where we stayed in Simon's home and courtyard free of charge. The house, being large enough for small gatherings of people and close to the synagogue, made an ideal base. As Jesus had already made me responsible for our limited supply of money, I was pleased with this economical arrangement.

For months we travelled around Galilee, learning from Jesus as he taught and healed. We relied upon people's generosity for food and shelter. I wasn't used to being without money, and found it very liberating. These were exciting times, full of hope. As Jesus's fame spread it became difficult for us to escape the crowds, but he always refused to send people away. I think he genuinely loved them all.

On one such occasion we were resting indoors. Jesus was deep in discussion with some Pharisees, strict teachers of Jewish law. Outside, as usual, a crowd was gathering. Suddenly, Simon leaped to his feet. 'What's that noise on the roof?'

We looked up to see a paralysed man being lowered from the roof on a stretcher.

His friends had found a way to reach Jesus through the crowds. Jesus seemed impressed by their faith. He touched the man, saying, 'Friend, your sins are forgiven.'

The Pharisees looked uncomfortable. They were men of God, and this seemed wrong to them. 'Surely only God can forgive sins,' they mused.

'You fail to see what true forgiveness looks like,' said Jesus, 'so you refuse to believe. Watch and believe.' Turning to the paralysed man, he said quietly, 'Take up your bed and walk.'

The man, amazed, did as he was bid.

As I said, exciting times.

One of the most exciting things about Jesus was that he was not afraid to challenge people, even figures of authority, about their beliefs and lifestyles. I convinced myself that these were small steps towards great change.

One afternoon we passed the booth of a tax collector called Levi. Tax collectors were hated by the Jewish people because they gave our money to the Romans, and mixed with non-Jews, which was forbidden by law.

Jesus called out to Levi those now familiar words, 'Follow me.' To the surprise of everyone around us, Levi immediately got up and ran to Jesus's side, leaving his money on the table. That evening Levi invited Jesus to join him and his friends, most of whom were also tax collectors, in a celebratory meal.

Some of the Pharisees heard about Levi, and challenged Jesus. 'Why do you eat and drink with sinners?' they asked, unsmiling.

Jesus explained, 'It is the sick who need a doctor, not the healthy. I am here to help sinners – the righteous do not need such help.' This was radical!

Jesus's actions plunged us into another area of controversy. Rabbis and Pharisees had for years been debating which of two contradictory demands should take precedence. Our laws tell us to rest on the Sabbath, but we also need to survive and to respond to people's needs.

I remember one Sabbath we were walking through a farmer's field. As we walked, we plucked a few ears of wheat, rubbed them to get rid of the chaff, and chewed the grain inside.

16

'Oh no, here's trouble,' muttered James, pointing to the edge of the field, where two Pharisees had stopped in their tracks to watch us. One of the Pharisees called out, 'Why are you harvesting on the Sabbath?'

I laughed, and muttered 'Don't be so ridiculous', but Jesus touched my arm to silence me. He approached the Pharisees.

He explained to them that looking after others, like feeding people when they are hungry, must sometimes take precedence over strict religious law. He reminded them that even famous King David had technically broken the law when he once fed his hungry men with the bread reserved for the Sabbath. He looked them in the eye. 'And I,' he said quietly, 'am lord of the Sabbath.'

This was very daring, some might say arrogant. This was exciting. Jesus was publicly claiming authority over the law.

Jesus also attracted criticism for healing

on the Sabbath, but it never stopped him. 'Is it really wrong to do good and to save life on the Sabbath?' he challenged those who questioned him.

He always knew what to say – unlike me.

One calm evening we were in the hills praying. Jesus drew twelve of us close to him. 'There is too much work for me to do alone,' he confided. 'Soon I must rely on you to tell people about me and heal the sick.'

I looked at the other eleven men. What a strange collection! We were from such varied backgrounds;

we had different strengths, different ideas.
Some of us were more driven, some – dare I
say it – more intelligent than others. I looked at
Simon, Andrew, James and John. They were only
fishermen. Could Jesus *really* rely on *all* of us?

As Jesus led us down to the crowd below, he put his arm around my shoulders. I swelled with pride that he was singling me out from the others. Perhaps he shared my doubts about their abilities. Perhaps this was his way of expressing special favour. In hindsight, however, I think he had read my mind and felt sorry for me.

Jesus began to preach. His words, though addressed to the crowd, held special significance for the twelve of us he had just chosen. 'Blessed are you who are poor,' he assured, 'for yours is the kingdom of God. Blessed are you who hunger, for you will be fed.' He taught that those who grieved would be comforted, and that the pure, the good and the peacemakers would all be welcomed by God. Looking meaningfully towards us, he affirmed 'Blessed are you when men hate you because of me.' A chill ran through me.

Though Jesus's message was straightforward, his demands were often difficult.

'Love your enemies,' he preached. 'If you only care for those who care for you, what credit is that to you? Even sinners can do that much! You must learn to treat everybody as you would like them to treat you. Forgive other people, and you will be forgiven.' He paused to take a sip of water, then looked meaningfully round the crowd. 'And be very careful not to judge others; if you do, you risk being judged in the same way.'

Was he looking at me when he said that? I shrank back a little, but he caught my eye. 'How is it that you people can comment so readily on the speck of dust in your brother's eye, yet manage to overlook the plank lodged in your own?'

Jesus followed this with a parable. Parables, apparently simple stories with a message that often seemed puzzling or shocking, were his way of helping ordinary people – including fishermen like Simon – to understand.

'The person who understands my words and puts them into practice is like a man who builds

a house with deep foundations on solid rock.
When the flood comes, the torrent strikes their
house, but because it is so well built the water
hardly shakes it. The person who understands my
words yet fails to live by them' – surely he wasn't
looking at me again – 'is like a man who builds a
house on the sand, with no foundations. As soon
as the torrent strikes, the house collapses.'

Did Jesus mean that, the moment trouble
comes, such an insecure man might also collapse?

22

Returning to the seashore at Capernaum, we were approached by some Jewish elders. 'A centurion's servant is sick, can you come and heal him?' Worried that Jesus might hesitate to help a Roman, they added, 'This centurion has been very good to our people,' but Jesus was already on his way. As we neared the centurion's house we met a messenger. Jesus read aloud what the centurion had written – 'I do not deserve to have you in my home. You do not need to come. Just say the word and my servant will be healed.'

Jesus turned to us. 'Let me tell you,' he said seriously, 'I have not found faith like this among my own people, let alone the Romans.'

A Roman with greater faith than a Jew? I wasn't sure how I felt about that. The next day, however, when we heard that the servant was well again, I was forced to reconsider.

All in all I was reconsidering a great deal. Most Pharisees, like my father, were good men, but they tended towards an inflexible adherence to Jewish law. I often felt sad when I thought of my father. I had left him because Jesus offered a more compassionate alternative. I remembered my early expectations that Jesus would challenge the authorities. I was beginning to grow less certain.

From Capernaum we travelled to Nain, where a Pharisee invited us to dine with him. As we ate, a woman entered the room and knelt beside Jesus. I recognised her face from the morning's crowd, where I had noticed her neighbours shunning her, whispering the word 'sinner'. Now, the weeping woman soaked Jesus's feet with tears which she wiped away with her hair. She then rubbed perfumed ointment onto his feet, and I heard her say quietly, 'Lord, please forgive my sins.'

It was rather embarrassing. I wondered how much she had paid for the ointment. She could have given the money to the poor instead. We watched in silence until the Pharisee said to Jesus, 'If you really were the messiah, you would know that this woman is a sinner.'

Jesus turned to him. I sighed – another parable. 'Two men owed money to a money lender. One owed five hundred coins, the other just fifty. Neither could afford to repay him, so he cancelled both their debts. Which of them was more grateful?'

'The one who had owed more, of course.'

'That's right,' replied Jesus. 'You didn't even offer me water to wash my feet when I arrived, but this woman washed my feet with her tears and dried them with her hair; she kissed my feet and anointed them with perfume. She had the least, but gave the most. She knows how to love, and her many sins have been forgiven.' He smiled at the woman. 'Your faith has saved you,' he said gently. 'Go in peace.'

I enjoyed the look of shock, or was it anger too, that I saw in the Pharisee's face.

We were gradually making our way south towards Jerusalem, teaching and healing in the towns on our way. Somewhere on our travels, Jesus had driven many demons out of a woman called Mary Magdalene. Since then, Mary and some of her friends had been financially supporting our work, and Mary often joined us. As I was still responsible for our money, I appreciated their help, although it felt strange to rely on women.

As I have already said, Jesus often taught in parables to help people think for themselves, and not just follow the laws blindly. I remember one parable about a man sowing grain. Some of the grain fell on rocky ground, where it could not take root, while some fell amongst weeds, which choked the young seedlings. Some grain, however, fell in good soil and grew well.

'I don't understand,' I remember Simon saying. 'What can I learn from that?'

'The grain sown on rocky ground is like people who hear the word of God but ignore it,' Jesus explained. 'The grain choked by weeds is like the people who hear what God says and try to live by it, but fail when the going gets too hard.' Why did he look at me; was it because he thought I might fail if *I* was tested? 'And, of course,' he smiled at Simon, 'the grain that grows well is like the people who hear what God has to say and have the strength and understanding to live up to it.'

On another occasion, a lawyer asked Jesus a question. 'You talk a lot about loving my neighbour,' he said, 'but who exactly is my neighbour? Just the people who live nearby?'

'A man was travelling from Jerusalem to Jericho,' began Jesus, 'when he was attacked by robbers who beat him, took everything he had, and left him naked and dying on the roadside. The first person to pass by was a Levite.' Levites were often temple assistants, people we respected. 'The Levite saw the wounded man, but he walked on without helping him. After a long time, just when the traveller was giving up hope, a Samaritan came along.' We all knew that most Jews dislike the people of Samaria, who have strange ways of worshipping and dress differently from us. 'Well,' Jesus continued, 'when the Samaritan saw the desperate traveller he stopped, bandaged his wounds, lent him his cloak, and took him to an inn, where he paid for him to be looked after.'

'So here is my question,' Jesus looked directly at the lawyer. 'Which do you think was the traveller's true neighbour? The supposedly friendly Levite, or the supposedly untrustworthy Samaritan?'

'I understand now,' said the lawyer humbly. 'Everyone is my neighbour.'

One day Jesus gathered the twelve of us together. 'You are now ready. Go and preach my message, and heal the sick. You have God's authority.'

As Jesus warned us about the dangers that we might face, I looked around the group. Some looked excited, others looked scared. Simon was listening intently like a faithful dog. It was difficult to imagine Simon teaching anyone anything. Though he was eager to please, he often struggled to understand what Jesus was saying.

That evening two sisters, Mary and Martha, invited us to dinner. Martha bustled around preparing food and making the house comfortable, but Mary knelt at Jesus's feet, listening carefully to his words. I noticed Martha looking increasingly exasperated. Eventually, her face red and her voice tight, she strode into the room. 'It isn't fair,' she said. 'My sister has left me to do all the work. Tell her she must help me.'

'Martha,' said Jesus, 'I understand that you have a lot to worry about, but Mary has identified the one thing that is really important. It will not be taken from her.'

This seemed rather unfair. Most of the things Martha was doing did need to be done, though I thought she could have left some of her jobs to listen to Jesus. I sympathised with Martha, because I was always the one who had to find money and food for our group to live on. Some of us are burdened with practicalities, even if we might prefer to concentrate on spiritual things.

That night, Jesus taught Mary and Martha the simple prayer he taught all his followers. 'Our father in heaven, holy is your name. Your kingdom will come and your will must be done. Give us each day our daily bread. Forgive us our sins as we forgive those who sin against us. Lead us not into temptation, and deliver us from evil. The kingdom, the power, and the glory are all yours, now and for ever.'

Prayer was more important than food to Jesus. He insisted that God would always respond to prayer. Just as a good parent provides a child with what is needed, he explained, so God will always provide for us. He taught us to base all our prayers on this one simple one, and to talk to God as a child would talk to a parent. What a contrast with the elaborate prayers the Pharisees taught!

Everything Jesus taught made sense, but I was troubled. What was his ultimate goal? He told us that when we reached Jerusalem he would suffer and die. What would be the point in that? We hadn't achieved anything significant yet, and time was running out.

More and more often, Jesus accused some of the Pharisees of wickedness. 'Woe to you experts in the law,' he warned. 'You ignore justice and hide the keys to heaven.' I agreed with him – after all, this was partly why I had left my father. Yet angering the Pharisees with accusations and insults seemed petty and counterproductive. Surely we should either work with the Pharisees to improve things, or confront them directly. The middle way we seemed to be adopting was simply frustrating.

As we continued towards Jerusalem, I felt an increasing sense of urgency. It was becoming more and more difficult to accept the passivity of Jesus's teaching.

I think we were in Pella when a man asked Jesus to help him sort out his inheritance issues with his brother. As so often, Jesus responded with a parable.

'A man worked hard and stored up wealth so that he could live more easily in the future. But it was all in vain, because he died while he was still gathering together enough money.' He turned to the small crowd that had gathered. 'Beware of all kinds of greed. You mustn't worry about what you will eat or what you will wear. Look at the birds. They do not sow or reap, yet God still feeds them, and you are much more valuable than birds. The lilies in the field do not make clothes, yet they are always dressed in splendour. If that is how God clothes the flowers, how much more will he clothe you? You have far too little faith! Give your possessions to the poor – your heavenly father will give you all that you need.'

This was reassuring, even inspiring, pointing us towards spiritual rather than tangible wealth. Nevertheless, if we were going to eat tonight I needed to go and find us some food. The words, clever though they were, were just words. What about some action?

Jesus had high expectations. He said that people should give up everything they had, including their family, to follow him. That's what I had done the day I turned my back on my father. Jesus also said that we should be prepared to die for him. A little more difficult, I thought. What can dying achieve?

But all in all, I enjoyed the simple lifestyle. I didn't need my father's wealth, and I never doubted the wisdom of Jesus's teaching. I grew to believe that Jesus was right to make God's forgiveness and love available to everyone.

'Suppose you had a hundred sheep, and lost one of them,' he taught one day. 'Would you not

leave the ninety-nine and keep looking for the lost sheep until you found it?'

People nodded.

'And when you found it, wouldn't you carry it home, overjoyed that the lost sheep was safe and well?'

More nods.

Jesus explained. 'There is more joy in heaven over one sinner who repents than ninety-nine good people who do not need to repent.'

He then told a story about a son who asked his father for his share of his inheritance, which he then wasted. This prodigal son, reduced to nothing, returned to his father, expecting to be punished. But his father was thrilled to see him, and organised a celebratory feast to welcome him home.

To Jesus, every sinner was a lost sheep, a prodigal son. He would bring them home.

Although we almost always travelled as a group, I sometimes felt lonely. There was no one with whom I could share my doubts and confusion about what we were trying to achieve. I had accepted that we weren't going to challenge Roman rule, but I was increasingly concerned that we didn't even seem to be moving towards direct confrontation with the Jewish authorities.

One day, Jesus asked us all who we thought he was. Simon immediately answered, 'You are the son of the living God.' Jesus was pleased, and from then on called Simon 'Peter', after the Greek word for 'rock'. 'Those who recognise who I am will be the rock on which I will build my church,' said Jesus. From then on, Simon Peter's confidence grew while mine seemed to diminish.

I remembered John the Baptist's promise, that a greater man was coming.

Was Jesus this man? I had never been sure, and still could not share the certainty enjoyed by the others. One day, somebody asked Jesus precisely when the kingdom of God would come on earth. At last, I thought, something specific.

'The kingdom of God is already within you', said Jesus. I sort of understood, but it was never quite enough. It was too internal. Jesus continued, 'The son of God will come like lightning flashing in the sky, but first he must suffer at the hands of his own generation.'

What did that mean? That his goals would only be achieved by his own death?

So much had happened since I first met Jesus, but nothing could have prepared me for the next few days. We finally reached the outskirts of Jerusalem. James and John found a colt for Jesus to ride into the city. We walked behind, singing psalms of expectation. But my heart was not in my song. My expectations were low.

Excited, optimistic crowds lined our route to the temple, joining our psalms and spreading palm branches in our path. The rest of the group were clearly exhilarated by our triumphal arrival in Jerusalem, and my mood improved. The psalms voiced Jewish hopes, and the palm is our national symbol. Perhaps the authorities would consider this a challenge. They must now feel threatened. Surely they would have to act.

When we reached the temple, Jesus looked in horror at what was going on there. It looked more like a market place than a temple. At dinner that evening, Jesus outlined a plan. 'We need to reclaim the temple as a place of prayer,' he said. My heartbeat quickened – he was going to mount a challenge!

All Jews had to pay temple tax and buy animals for sacrifice. For both we needed special silver coins. The only place to exchange our money for these coins was the temple, and the exchange rate was weighted heavily in favour of the money-changers. The poor were being robbed – in the temples.

As Jesus explained his plan, my father's words echoed in my head – 'He will cause division.' I felt a thrill of anticipation, swiftly and confusingly followed by a heavy sense of dread.

When we arrived at the temple the next morning, we found an elderly woman trying to exchange her money. She wept as the money-changer refused to give her a fair rate. Jesus approached the table. I held my breath, awed by his controlled anger. Using very little force, Jesus simply lifted the side of the table, sending the silver coins clattering across the floor. The money-changer stared, open-mouthed.

We knew what we had to do. We crashed other tables onto their sides; coins cascaded to the ground. We overturned the benches of men selling doves for sacrifice. Action at last! We caused chaos! Animals ran wild. Money-dealers scrabbled around on the ground, trying to catch their clattering coins. Angry men tried to stop us; others cheered us on. Violence seemed inevitable.

In the midst of the chaos, Jesus strode to the top of the steps. His authoritative voice silenced the din. 'Is it not written in the scriptures that the temple should be a house of prayer for all the nations? You have turned it into a den of thieves!' Noticing a large group of priests moving threateningly towards him, Jesus warned his listeners, 'Do not allow yourselves to be turned away from God.'

In the tense silence that followed, I was surprised to recognise a priest standing next to me. It was Zacharias, one of my father's friends. 'Well, Judas,' he smirked, 'that was rather dramatic. You must be pleased.'

I nodded, my jaw tense.

'Of course, it will make no difference.'

'Maybe not immediately,' I muttered through gritted teeth, 'but soon we shall free our people from oppression.'

'You fool,' sneered Zacharias. 'Jesus and his naive ideas will never challenge any authority.

Have you followed him for three years without understanding his words? Haven't you heard him say, "My kingdom is not of this world," and "give to Caesar what belongs to Caesar"?'

I was stunned. Zacharias was right. All along Jesus had been telling us that real change comes from within us, not from outside. But I hadn't wanted to hear.

'Jesus will never make any real difference,' continued Zacharias. 'In fifty years, no one will even remember his name. Or yours.'

I unclenched my fists and walked away. I needed to think.

Jesus preached in the temple for several days. Afraid to confront such a popular man, the priests tried to catch him out with trick questions. Jesus always silenced them with his answers. This intellectual sparring was clever, but it left me feeling empty. Words, words, words.

When I had believed that Jesus would match his words with action, I had applauded everything he said, but now I was worried. Hundreds of people were leaving their families to follow Jesus, just as I had done, and giving away all that they owned. People were suffering in order to follow him. For what purpose? What suffering lay ahead for those who continued to follow him? I began to feel that Jesus needed to be stopped, both for his own sake and for the safety of his followers.

Zacharias sought me out. 'Your friend is dangerous,' he frowned. 'He must be stopped.' This reflected my own thoughts so closely that I was shocked. Zacharias's frown melted into a smile. 'Come and talk to my friends.'

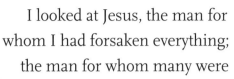

I looked at Jesus, the man for whom I had forsaken everything; the man for whom many were prepared to die; the man who was unlikely to achieve anything unless forced into direct confrontation; the man who had chosen Simon as his 'rock'.

The familar feelings of disappointment, longing and jealousy were too painful.

I turned my back on him and followed Zacharias into the temple.

The time to celebrate the Passover arrived, but I didn't feel celebratory. Days before, in return for thirty pieces of silver, I had promised the priests that I would find them an opportunity to arrest Jesus. That should force him into action. If not, at least his dangerous inaction would be stopped.

Jesus sent Simon Peter and John to find and prepare a room for our meal that night. As usual it was my job to provide the food. It was a cosy room that they found, just big enough for the thirteen of us, with a low table and couches on three sides. Jesus invited me to share his couch, a place of honour. I felt very uncomfortable, knowing what I had to do.

Before we ate, Jesus said, 'I am pleased to eat this Passover meal with you all before I have to suffer.' I shivered. Jesus's references to his future suffering took on a new meaning now I had made my deal with the temple priests.

Jesus picked up some bread and gave thanks for it. Giving us each a piece, he said, 'This is my body, given for you. Do this to remember me.' He then picked up the cup of wine. 'This is God's new promise to you, in my blood.'

I dipped my bread into the wine with Jesus, then rested

46

my hand upon the table alongside his and John's. Quiet moments passed before Jesus said softly, 'The hand of the man who will betray me is with mine on the table.' I quickly moved my hand away. 'Woe to that man who betrays me,' he said quietly.

John was horrified. 'Is it me?' he asked.

I felt dizzy. I could not look at Jesus. 'Surely not me, Rabbi?'

Jesus whispered into my ear, 'I shall go to the Mount of Olives afterwards to pray.'

He knew! He knew what I was going to do! After the meal I stumbled down the stairs. Tears blurred my vision and emotion blurred my thoughts. I ran to where the chief priest lived. I kept my promise.

'We need you with us, to identify him,' insisted a guard.

'No, please, no!'

It was a miserable walk to the Mount of Olives. The moon was bright, and the guards were noisy in their armour. Jesus must have seen and heard us. I'm sure he could have escaped if he had wanted to. I wish that he had.

When we arrived he was standing calmly, waiting. Then I saw the others. Simon Peter was rubbing his eyes as if he had been asleep.

A guard pushed me roughly forward. 'Rabbi!' I greeted Jesus, identifying him in just one word. Then I kissed his cheek.

'Judas,' he smiled, 'do you hand me over with a kiss?'

The dreamlike, dreadful stillness was suddenly broken. The disciples and the guards prepared to fight, but Jesus raised his hand to calm them. He asked the priests sadly, 'Is it because I am leading a rebellion that you have come with swords? I was with you in the temple courts every day, yet you did not lay a hand on me. Now darkness reigns, and this is your hour.' Then he allowed himself to be led away. His friends fled. I wanted to run, but the guards held me.

The hours that followed were the worst of my life. I hadn't given much thought to what might happen to Jesus. I suppose I had hoped that my actions would make Jesus do something decisive, something that would really change things. Instead, I had to watch while he endured the most sickening brutality. The guards insulted him and beat him. They blindfolded him, hit him and taunted him.

Why didn't he save himself? I struggled to convince myself that there were good reasons for what I had done.

It was daybreak when they tried Jesus. 'Are you really the son of God?' they asked.

'You say that I am,' answered Jesus.

That was enough. 'Blasphemy!' cried the chief priest triumphantly. 'We have heard it from his own lips! What more do we need? Take him to Pilate!'

Pontius Pilate was the Roman prefect of the province. I followed as they led Jesus to Pilate's palace. 'This man opposes the payment of taxes to Caesar and claims to be a messiah, a king,' the priests told Pilate. I gasped at their lies. The irony struck me with terrible force. I had betrayed this selfless, compassionate man because he had failed to do either of the things of which he was now accused.

Pilate looked carefully at Jesus. 'Are you the King of the Jews?'

'So you say.'

Pilate turned to the priests and the crowd that had followed. 'I find no basis for a charge against him.'

This caused uproar, the priests insisting that Jesus had tried to stir up rebellion. Pilate, growing uncomfortable, continued to argue that there was no charge to be answered. Eventually, seeking to pass the burden of responsibility to somebody else, Pilate sent Jesus to King Herod, who was in Jerusalem for the Passover. Herod sent Jesus straight back to Pilate. Wearily, Pilate addressed the crowd outside his palace. 'I find no basis for charges against this man. Neither does Herod. To appease you, I will punish him then release him, but I will not kill him.'

The crowd roared its dissatisfaction. Why was I being forced to endure this? I tried not to catch Jesus's eye. I had kept my promise. Seeing Jesus humiliated was dreadful; seeing the way he looked at me was far, far worse. I wanted to return my money to the priests, to undo what I had done. It was too late.

Alongside Jesus stood another prisoner, Barabbas, a rebel accused of murder. Pilate turned to the crowd. 'I will release one of these men. You must choose who will be freed.' I shared Pilate's undisguised hope that they would release Jesus; that this terrible course of events would end, but the crowd's chant of 'Release Barabbas, release Barabbas' was as deafening as it was shocking. The mounting hysteria became more bloodthirsty, the chant changing to 'Crucify Jesus!' My whole body shook. Crucifixion!

Pilate tried to quieten them. 'Why?' he asked.

He was answered with a crescendo of chanting – 'Crucify him!' Pilate had no choice. Symbolically, he asked for a basin of water to wash his hands of the whole business.

Had I had a choice? Could I now, like Pilate, wash the guilt from my hands?

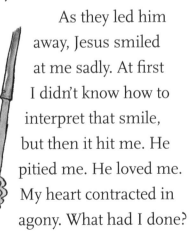

As they led him away, Jesus smiled at me sadly. At first I didn't know how to interpret that smile, but then it hit me. He pitied me. He loved me. My heart contracted in agony. What had I done?

They killed him this afternoon. The sky grew as dark as my soul.

How can I live with such guilt? Can I find comfort in the possibility that this was God's plan, that I had no choice? Maybe our goals will be better served by Jesus's death than by his life, as he so often hinted. Is this how he will bring his lost sheep home? I don't fully understand.

Or perhaps Zacharias's words will turn out to be true – 'He will never make any real difference. In fifty years no one will even remember his name. Or yours.'

I will not be there to find out.

TAKING THINGS FURTHER

The real read

This *Real Reads* volume of *Judas Iscariot* is our interpretation of the events of the New Testament, told from the perspective of one of the most significant participants. In writing this account of Judas's life, we have used evidence from the gospel according to Luke. This is one of the four gospels – the first four books of the New Testament.

It is important to acknowledge that all four gospels were written after Jesus's death, and that the writers had different aims in mind – although they all wanted to engender faith in the reader that Jesus was the Son of God. The first three gospels – Matthew, Mark and Luke – are called 'the synoptic gospels'. They were probably written between forty and sixty years after the crucifixion. The gospel according to John, written later, is significantly different.

Sometimes, the four gospels' accounts of events differ considerably. At first this made our task rather difficult, until we realised that what we needed to do was present the New Testament as it is, rather than to weave a path of our choice between the gospels. Therefore, if you read all six books in the *Real Reads* New Testament series, you may well notice some of the apparent contradictions and inconsistencies that are present in the Bible itself.

There is a gospel of Judas, discovered in Egypt in the 1970s. Although a great deal of controversy surrounds this text, it has been radiocarbon dated to around the late third century. We considered drawing upon evidence from the gospel of Judas for this *Real Reads* version, but decided that our job was to stay faithful to the recognised New Testament.

As with all the other characters in this series, we do not really know what Judas thought of the events through which he lived. Using thorough research and paying close attention to the Bible account, we have tried to imagine what he might have been like, and what he might have thought.

This *Real Reads Judas Iscariot* does not cover all the events of the New Testament. Reading the other five books in the series will bring you closer to an understanding of the complete story. You may then want to read the New Testament itself. We recommend that you read either the *New International Version* or *The Youth Bible*, details of which are given below.

Biblical sources

Although *Judas Iscariot* is based on the story as told in the gospel of Luke, there are a few places where we have drawn on other sources.

On the *Real Reads* website you will find an online concordance (www.realreads.co.uk/newtestament/concordance/judas). A 'bible concordance' is an indexing tool which allows you to see how the same words, sentences and passages appear in different versions and translations of the Bible. This online concordance will direct you from events in the *Real Reads* version back to their biblical sources, so you can see clearly where each part of our story is drawn from.

Life in
New Testament times

The main events of Judas's life took place in
Palestine, a long narrow area of land bordered
to the west by the Mediterranean Sea and to the
east by the Transjordanian Desert. Some parts
of Palestine were desert, some were hill country,
some rich pasture land, and some uncultivated
wilderness.

The Jews considered Palestine to be their
'promised land', promised to them by God. Moses
had led them there from slavery in Egypt. The
area was mainly Jewish, with synagogues and
temples. Nevertheless, it is interesting that most
of Jesus's ministry took place around the Sea of
Galilee, an area with a mixed population of Jews
and Gentiles, and a reputation for political unrest.

Although Palestine was Jewish land, it was
part of the Roman Empire and under Roman
control. The Jews resented paying taxes to
Rome. During Jesus's lifetime, there was
considerable conflict between the Jews and their

N
W   E
S

Capernaum ●

SEA
OF
GALILEE

GALILEE

Nazareth ●

Nain ●

Pella ●

SAMARIA

RIVER JORDAN

PALESTINE

Jericho ●

Jerusalem ●

Bethany ●

10   20 miles

DEAD
SEA

Roman rulers. Some Jews must have hoped that Jesus would help to overthrow the Romans. This helps to explain why the Romans might have been nervous of the crowds following Jesus.

The Romans used the existing Jewish authorities to help to govern their subjects. This gave further power and influence to the Jewish leaders. As with any group given such powers, some of these leaders used their influence for the good of the people, some used it corruptly.

Jews of the time, as is still the case for many orthodox Jews today, followed very strict laws, which Judas would have studied as a boy. The Old Testament tells the story of how these laws, the Torah, were handed down from God to Moses. Pharisees were teachers of the law who felt responsible for ensuring that people kept the laws. The Pharisees were very concerned when Jesus seemed to challenge the Torah, though many ordinary Jews would have welcomed the promise of a less authoritative regime.

Finding out more

We recommend the following books and websites to gain a greater understanding of the New Testament.

Books

We strongly recommend that you read the rest of the *Real Reads* New Testament series, as the six narratives interlock to give a more complete picture of events. These are *Jesus of Nazareth, Mary of Galilee, Simon Peter, Mary Magdalene* and *Paul of Tarsus*.

- *New Century Youth Bible*, Authentic Lifestyle, 2007.

- Sally Lloyd-Jones, *The Jesus Storybook Bible: Every Story Whispers his Name*, Zondervan, 2007.

- *People in the Life of Jesus*, Colin Lumsden, Day One Publications, 2003.

- Stephen Adly Guirgis, *The Last Days of Judas Iscariot*, Methuen, 2008.

Websites

- www.bbc.co.uk/religion/religions/christianity/history/whokilledjesus_1.shtml
This interesting and accessible assessment of the parties involved suggests that Judas's involvement was less important than is often accepted.

- www.gospel-mysteries.net/judas-iscariot.html
Some interesting possibilities about Judas.

- www.localhistories.org/new
Brief but useful descriptions of many aspects of everyday life in New Testament times.

TV and film

- *Jesus Christ Superstar*, directed by Norman Jewison. Universal Pictures UK, 2005. This screen version of the 1970s rock opera by Tim Rice and Andrew Lloyd Webber focuses on the relationship between Jesus and Judas.

- *Jesus of Nazareth*, directed by Franco Zeffirelli. ITV DVD, 1977. A six and a half hour mini-series.

Food for thought

Here are some things to think about if you are reading *Judas Iscariot* alone, ideas for discussion if you are reading it with friends.

Starting points

● How would you describe Judas before he decides to follow Jesus? Why can't he decide what to do with his life?

● The words 'longing', 'disappointment' and 'jealousy' appear on pages 8 and 45. Why do you think Judas is experiencing these feelings so strongly on each occasion?

● Can you find examples of Judas's admiration and love for Jesus?

● Can you find examples of Judas's hopes and expectations concerning Jesus?

● What does Judas think about Simon Peter?

- List some of the lessons Jesus teaches people. Can you think of examples of what these lessons might mean in everyday life?

- What evidence is there that Judas became disappointed with Jesus?

- How did you feel about Judas at the end of the book?

Group activities

- With a group of friends, act out the Passover meal in Jerusalem. Give each other advice on how the characters were feeling.

- Imagine Judas's conversation with Zacharias when he follows him into the temple. Can you write it as a short drama and act it out?

- Starting on page 45, take turns reading to the end of the book. Whoever is reading is Judas. Stop at different points in the story and interview Judas about his feelings at that point.

SIMON PETER

www.realreads.co.uk

Retold by Alan Moore and Gill Tavner
Illustrated by Karen Donnelly

Published by Real Reads Ltd
Stroud, Gloucestershire, UK
www.realreads.co.uk

First published in 2010

ISBN 978-1-906230-26-5

Printed in China by Imago Ltd
Designed by Lucy Guenot
Typeset by Bookcraft Ltd, Stroud, Gloucestershire

CONTENTS

THE CHARACTERS

Simon Peter

Simon is a simple fisherman. What qualities does Jesus see in him? Can Simon learn enough from his weaknesses to be able to do the work that Jesus has in mind for him?

Jesus

Simon's love for Jesus is unlimited and unquestioning. What will Jesus demand of Simon? Will Simon ever let him down?

Judas

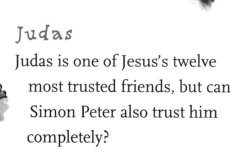

Judas is one of Jesus's twelve most trusted friends, but can Simon Peter also trust him completely?

Mary Magdalene

When Jesus heals Mary Magdalene, she becomes an important supporter of his work. What startling news will she bring to Simon Peter?

Pontius Pilate

Pilate is the Roman governor of the province. He offers to release a prisoner, but who will it be?

Stephen

Stephen proves himself a brave and virtuous man. Will Simon ever be as brave as him?

Paul

Paul is well known for persecuting Jesus's followers, but now claims to have changed his mind. Should Simon Peter trust him?

SIMON PETER

Catching fish. That's what Andrew and I were doing on the day that changed our lives for ever. That was what we had always done; it was what our father and our grandfather had always done. For generations we had lived as fishermen in the village of Capernaum, by the Sea of Galilee. Until that day, we had no expectation of ever doing anything else.

We were good Jews. We respected the Sabbath, Jewish festivals and Jewish laws. Until that day, we thought this was the way to satisfy God. How wrong we were. He wanted so much more.

The day started like any other. Having cast our nets into the lake, Andrew and I were beginning to relax, drifting just offshore. Waiting.

'Hey!' We looked up. A man was calling, and beckoning to us from the shore.

'Simon, who is that?' asked Andrew. 'Isn't it Jesus?'

I wasn't sure. It looked like Jesus, who we had seen a few times in town, but we were still quite far from the shore. We pulled in our nets, sailed back, and beached the boat.

Jesus looked at us. We looked at him. Though nobody spoke, we didn't feel awkward. I felt a great sense of peace, rather like the period immediately after casting the nets. It was Jesus who broke the silence. 'Come, leave your nets. I will make you fishers of people.'

We must have looked like caught fish ourselves as we stared at him open-mouthed. He seemed amused. 'Follow me,' he invited, turning away.

Looking back, it's hard to remember quite what made us decide to follow him, but we did. Just like that.

Jesus invited our neighbours, James and John, to follow him too. From that day we all stayed together. Jesus taught us and trusted us. Other people joined us. Eventually, from

the growing crowd, Jesus selected eight other
men to help him. We were from a range of
backgrounds – there were even tax collectors,
and one man, Judas, was the son of a priest. He
was better educated than most of us, as he often
liked to point out. Jesus entrusted Judas with
responsibility for our money.

There were many other followers, but Jesus relied upon us twelve.

We followed Jesus around Galilee. He taught in synagogues, by the lakeside, and on mountaintops – anywhere that people gathered. News of his preaching spread quickly, and he was soon attracting huge crowds. He made it clear that he had come to help the poor, the weak and the suffering. Looking back, I can see that it was so simple, but at the time I often misunderstood what he was telling us.

You may wonder why so many people wanted to hear Jesus. Well, some wanted to learn from him; others were simply curious. Many hoped that Jesus would lead a revolt against the Romans, or change the Jewish laws, the Torah. However, he insisted that he had come to fulfil the Torah rather than abolish it. Jesus taught that our love of God should show in how we treat other people, even the Romans. We should help the poor and the weak, and we should love and forgive our enemies. Jesus always closed with the same simple prayer, then sent his listeners to go and live in the way he had taught.

Sick people came to Jesus to be healed. He made lame people walk; he cured lepers; he even made dead people live again. In the early days, when we were still in Capernaum, he cured my mother-in-law of a fever.

On another occasion he healed a woman, Mary Magdalene, who was possessed by demons. After this, Mary committed herself to Jesus's work.

She was a wealthy woman, and her support was very useful to us. She sometimes joined us on our travels, which seemed strange at first, but I soon got used to her.

Jesus expected a great deal more of his twelve close followers than he expected of anybody else. One evening, he drew us together. 'I have work for you to do,' he said. 'There's too much for me alone. Go, preach my message, heal the sick. You now have God's authority.'

Perhaps we looked a little too pleased, because he warned us, 'People will hate you and try to kill you because of me.' This was frightening, but I have never forgotten his next words. 'Although they may hurt your body, if you stand firm to the end, they cannot kill your soul.'

The work was exhausting for us all, but especially for Jesus, who never stopped. Once, after a particularly busy day when we hadn't even had time to eat, Jesus appeared sad and weary. He gave us the news that John the Baptist, a holy man and Jesus's friend, had been beheaded by King Herod.

'I need time alone to pray,' Jesus told us.

We helped him into a boat on Galilee. Although we tried to do this discreetly, we couldn't stop the noisy crowds following him along the shore. Later that evening, we caught up with them. Jesus had left his boat and found a small hill on which to stand and teach. Although it was growing late, over five thousand men, women and children were still listening intently. They must all have been as hungry as we were.

Andrew nudged Jesus. 'We should let them go to the village for food.'

'No,' replied Jesus. 'Feed them here.' We looked at each other. We only had five loaves and two fish between us. This wouldn't feed us, let alone five thousand people.

'Do you really want me to go and spend two

hundred silver coins on bread for them all?' asked Judas, incredulous.

Jesus took a loaf. Looking up to heaven, he thanked God, broke the bread into pieces, and gave it to us to distribute. I looked at the basket and looked at the crowds. This wouldn't go very far!

I gave a small piece to a man, the same to another. Having anxiously fed a few people in this way, I began to notice that the food in my basket, rather than diminishing, was increasing. No matter how much food I took out, my basket always seemed to be full. I looked over at Thaddeus, who was feeding another group.

The same thing was happening there.

When the crowds had eventually dispersed, we found ourselves left with twelve baskets full of food. I sat next to Jesus. 'You knew, didn't you?'

Jesus was laughing. 'Help yourselves.'

That night, leaving Jesus to enjoy his longed-for solitude, the twelve of us took a boat out onto the lake. The water was calm, but the clouds threatened a storm. As an experienced fisherman, I offered to stay awake and keep an eye on the weather. The hours slipped slowly by, and the wind strengthened. As I stared sleepily across the water, I was chilled by an eerie vision. Something white, perhaps a spirit, was drifting towards us over the choppy water.

'Don't be afraid,' a voice called. 'It's me, Jesus.' Jesus reached out his hand to me. 'Come, Simon.'

I stepped gingerly out of the boat. I was walking on water. A miracle! But the mocking wind buffeted me. Walking on water? The wind howled with laughter. Impossible!

Doubt soaked through my clothes with the spray. I began to sink. 'Lord, save me!' I called.

Jesus reached out his hand and caught me. 'Oh, you of little faith.' He frowned. 'Why did you doubt?'

I had disappointed Jesus. It was frustrating. I always tried so hard, but I seemed to make more mistakes than the others. I needed more than my fair share of Jesus's patience.

Jesus told many short stories, or parables. Desperate to understand them, I often asked him to explain. I remember him once sighing wearily, 'Simon, do you still not understand?' But he always explained gently and kindly.

I still feel astonished that Jesus chose me, that amongst all his followers he decided that I should be the foundation for the future. We were in the region of Caesarea Philippi when it happened.

'Who do people say I am?' he asked us.

'Some say you are John the Baptist,' answered James, 'or a prophet.'

'Who do you say I am?' Jesus seemed to be looking at me.

'You are Christ, the son of the living God,' I answered.

Jesus nodded. 'Simon, you are blessed, because this was revealed to you by God. From now on I shall call you Peter, which means "rock". On this rock I will build my church and no evil shall overcome it. I will give you the keys of the kingdom of heaven, where you must show the same love and compassion that have been shown to you.'

Was he mocking me? I was probably the least rock-like person I had ever known. The others seemed as dumbfounded as I was. Jesus told us to sit down at the roadside. 'Do not tell anyone who I am,' he warned us. 'I must soon go to Jerusalem where I will be judged and put to death. Three days later I will rise from the dead.'

Horrified, appalled, I jumped up. 'No! No! That mustn't happen!'

Jesus looked at me sternly. 'Get behind me,

Satan! You are a stumbling block to me; you have in mind the things of men, not the things of God.'

I felt ashamed. Again.

Later I approached Jesus. 'How can I be a rock?'

'You love God. You love me.'

'But I make more mistakes than all of the others put together.'

'Because you try, you make mistakes. Because you make mistakes, you will grow.'

Several days later we were in the mountains. Jesus asked John, James and me to accompany him to the top of one of them. Hot and thirsty, we finally reached the summit. Jesus seemed to have something on his mind, and wandered away. We collapsed on the ground. Then the strangest thing happened. We watched in wonder as he became bathed in a strange light. His face and clothes shone like sunlight. Then two equally bright figures appeared beside him. They were Moses

and Elijah. I didn't know what to do. Trembling
with terror, I offered, 'Lord, we will make three
shelters – one for each of you.'

Jesus didn't respond. Then a cloud
enveloped the three of them, and a voice
rumbled all around us. 'This is my own dear
son – listen to him.'

We threw ourselves down in fear. Jesus came over and touched us gently, telling us not to be afraid. When we looked up, he was alone again.

It was hard to find the right words to talk about what had happened, so we descended the mountain in silence. Near the bottom, Jesus instructed us, 'Don't tell anyone what you have seen here until I have risen from the dead.'

In the following weeks, Jesus continued to refer to what lay ahead. He would be killed, he would rise again, and the kingdom of God would come. I don't think any of us really understood. I decided not to ask questions.

Jesus continued his work, whilst we still struggled to understand. One day, Judas asked, 'Master, who is the greatest in the kingdom of heaven?'

As so often, Jesus's answer sounded contradictory. 'Whoever wants to be first,' he

replied, 'must place himself last and be the
servant of all.' Some children were playing nearby.
Jesus called one of them over to him. Crouching
beside the boy, Jesus said,
'Whoever welcomes one of
these children in my
name welcomes me.
Whoever welcomes
me, welcomes God.'

   On another
occasion, some
mothers asked
Jesus to bless their
babies. We were concerned that Jesus had done
enough for one day, and started to usher them
away. But Jesus stopped us. 'Bring the children
to me. The kingdom of God belongs to such as
        these.' Tired though he was, he took
        the babies in his arms and blessed
        them.
        I think I understood this time.

To him, children represented the powerless, the voiceless, those most in need of kindness and protection.

Jesus's preaching could be both simple and complex at the same time. I remember a young man who approached Jesus, and anxiously asked him, 'Teacher, what must I do to receive eternal life?'

'Obey the commandments,' was Jesus's simple answer.

'Which ones?'

'Do not murder; do not commit adultery; do not steal; do not lie; respect your father and mother; and love your neighbour as yourself.'

'Master,' the man said, 'I have kept these. What else must I do?'

Jesus looked at him with love. 'Give all your possessions to the poor. Then come and follow me.' The young man's face fell; from his clothes we could see that he was quite wealthy. He walked away, deep in thought.

Jesus turned to us. 'Everybody has something which blocks their relationship with God. For that young man, it is his riches. To enter the kingdom of God, you must put God first, over everything else.'

How did this apply to us? 'We have given up everything,' I said. 'What is our reward?'

'You will reign with God, showing the same love and compassion to others as you have been shown. Everybody who puts God first, even above home and family, will receive eternal life.' A fine promise, but still I was haunted by the future Jesus had foreseen for himself here on earth.

The time came to travel to Jerusalem. Some of our group thought that this might be the beginning of Jesus's challenge to the power of Herod and Rome. Perhaps we were going to set up a new government run on holy principles. I wasn't so sure. Jesus had already warned us that he was fulfilling the scriptures; that horrors lay ahead. I heard my friends' hopes, but I couldn't share them.

The journey took several days. As we wearily approached Jerusalem, Jesus sent James and John ahead to the next village. 'You will find a donkey tied up there. Tell the owner that the master needs it.' When they returned, we put our cloaks on the donkey's back and Jesus mounted. He led us into Jerusalem.

Just as is written in the scriptures, crowds lined the streets, shouting psalms of expectation and cheering. 'Hosanna in the highest! Blessed is he who comes in the name of the Lord!'

Many pulled down palm branches, which they waved or spread before us. The palm is a national emblem, a sign of patriotism. The crowd's emotional reaction must have made the authorities feel very nervous. Perhaps my friends were right. This could be the beginning of an uprising.

At night, we left the city and slept in a nearby village called Bethany. The next morning we returned to Jerusalem's temple. Jesus had been angry since we visited the temple the day before. Once there, he overturned a money-lender's table. Following Jesus's lead, we caused chaos, overturning tables and benches, and releasing animals destined for sacrifice. In the middle of the confusion, Jesus called out, 'It is written, "My house shall be called a house of prayer," but you have made it a den of thieves.'

We had made a bold statement and upset many people. Trouble lay ahead. The Romans would be nervous about a possible uprising. The temple authorities would see Jesus as a direct challenge.

Indeed, in the following days, whenever Jesus taught in the temple, the priests' anger was evident in their faces, but they were powerless to act against Jesus in front of so many people. A riot would threaten their own positions. I noticed Judas talking with one of the priests. Judas looked uncomfortable.

The period of Passover arrived, normally a time for celebration and thanksgiving. On the first day of the festival, Jesus sent us towards a particular part of the city. 'You will find a man with a room. Tell him to prepare his room; we will celebrate the Passover at his house.'

That evening, Jesus was unusually quiet. The mood at the dinner table was sombre, not the happy family atmosphere we used to have at home on these occasions. I asked Jesus what was wrong.

'One of you here will betray me.'

'Who?' asked John. We were all anxious to know who it could possibly be.

Jesus spoke over our noise. 'One who dips his hand in the bowl with me.'

I noticed a swift movement to Jesus's right. Was it Judas? Did he move his hand away from the bowl? 'Surely not I, Rabbi?' I heard him ask.

Jesus whispered something to him. Poor Judas turned pale. A few minutes later, he left the room.

Jesus picked up some bread, thanked God for it, and broke it into pieces. He gave each of us a piece. 'Take and eat, this is my body.' Then he picked up the cup of wine, gave thanks, and passed that around too. 'Drink this, all of you. This is my blood, God's new promise, poured out for many for the forgiveness of sins. I will never again drink this wine until I am in my father's kingdom.'

I exchanged glances with the rest of the group. Was the dreaded time so close at hand?

Later that evening, Jesus wanted to go to the Garden
of Gethsemane, outside the city walls. I think he felt
that there he would find the peace, and the strength,
for prayer. It was already dark, but the moon was
bright. The walk took us through the eerie tombs of
the Kidron Valley, darkening our spirits further. As
we walked, Jesus sighed. 'Tonight, you will all flee
from me. After I am raised to life I will return to
Galilee ahead of you.'

I felt hurt. 'I'll never leave you, master, even if
the others do.'

'Peter,' Jesus sounded sad, 'before the cock
crows tonight, you will deny three times that you
know me.'

'I'll never deny you, even if I have to die with
you,' I insisted. 'Never.'

Jesus didn't respond.

Jesus took just three of us into the garden
with him. I looked closely at the face I loved so well.

I had never
seen him
so troubled.
He asked us
to keep watch
while he went to
pray. We tried, really we did, but when Jesus returned,
he found us all asleep. 'Couldn't you stay awake with
me for just one hour?' He seemed disappointed. 'I'll
go again. Pray that you don't fall asleep this time. Your
spirit is willing, but your flesh is weak.'

I fixed my eyes on Jesus. Sweat ran down his face
as he prayed. We prayed too, as he had directed, but
prayer lulled us back to sleep. Again, Jesus returned
to find us sleeping. We were ashamed. This happened
a third time, but when Jesus woke us this time he
seemed at last to be at peace with himself. 'Are you
still sleeping?' he smiled. 'Enough! The hour has
come! Look, here is the man who betrays me.'

Judas arrived with armed men. 'Greetings,
teacher,' he said, stepping forward and kissing Jesus.

Jesus looked directly at him. 'Friend, do what you came for.' Unbelievable! How could he call Judas 'friend'? They arrested Jesus. I prepared to fight, but Jesus stopped me. He turned to his captors. 'Why did you come with swords to capture me? I was with you in the temple every day and you did nothing.'

They took him away, a figure of calm in the chaos.

'Run!' urged Matthew. 'We'll regroup in Bethany.' I stayed. I had promised not to leave Jesus. I followed the soldiers to the house of Caiaphas, the high priest. Covering my head, I crept into the courtyard and sank into the shadows.

The priests challenged Jesus. 'Are you the son of God?'

He answered quietly, 'It is as you say.' They accused him of blasphemy and beat him. I knew that I would be in great danger if anybody recognised me as Jesus's friend. I was terrified, but I couldn't leave him. I hoped the darkness would hide me.

A serving-woman sidled close to me. 'Weren't you with Jesus of Galilee?' she whispered.

'I don't know what you're talking about,' I said, and moved away from her.

Then a girl, talking with others in a group, pointed to me. 'That man was with Jesus of Galilee!'

'I swear I don't know this man you're talking about.' I moved away again.

The group wouldn't leave me alone, and followed me. 'You are, you're one of his friends from Galilee,' another girl observed. 'You have a Galilean accent.'

Terrified, I shouted, 'I swear I don't know him! May God punish me if I lie!'

The tense silence following my outburst was broken by the crowing of a cock. I remembered Jesus's words. My tears of shame and grief tasted bitter.

Early the next morning, I learned that the Council of Priests had condemned Jesus to death and had handed him over to the Roman governor, Pontius Pilate. As I hurriedly joined the crowds outside the palace, Pilate appeared on the balcony. Behind him, his guards shoved Jesus and another prisoner.

Priests were slithering amongst the crowd, whispering venom. 'Jesus is a fraud,' they sneered. 'He said he was the messiah. He was going to liberate us Jews from the Romans. Now look at him!'

I looked. I wept inwardly. Brutally cut and bruised, Jesus looked exhausted.

Then Pilate addressed the crowd. 'Here is Jesus, who some of you call the anointed, and here is Barabbas, a murderer and thief. As it is your feast

of Passover,
I will release
a prisoner of
your choice.'

There was
a moment of quiet.
Here was hope. I held my breath. A man near me
shouted, 'Release Barabbas!'

I stood, appalled, as the crowd joined his chant.
I turned to the man. 'Why Barabbas?'

'He's a freedom fighter,' he replied, 'not like
this ineffective Jesus.' He turned back to face the
balcony. 'Crucify him!' he shouted.

This was insane! Pilate looked as perplexed as
I felt. 'Why?' he called. Receiving no reply other
than a crescendo of 'Crucify him,' Pilate washed his
hands and held them up to the crowd. 'This man's
blood is on your hands, not mine.'

Later that morning Roman soldiers nailed Jesus to a cross.

The moment Jesus died, the earth shook. Everything around us and everything within me shook. When stillness returned, the world was different. And so was I.

Jesus was dead. His followers were in great danger. I hurried through back streets to a friend's house. James and John were already there. Shocked and ashamed, we didn't know what to say to each other. I feared that all we had strived for over the last three years had failed. We didn't know that our work had only just begun.

We tried to observe the Sabbath, but our hearts were broken.

Word came that one of Jesus's followers, a man called Joseph of Aramethea, had taken Jesus's body and had placed it in his own tomb. We couldn't do anything about a proper burial on the Sabbath, but tomorrow we would attend to it. That night, the earth shook again.

Early the next morning, I was wakened by a loud banging at the door. Mary Magdalene was outside, shouting my name. 'His body has gone!' she gasped.

'What do you mean, gone?'

'The stone blocking the tomb has been rolled aside. We found an angel sitting on the stone. He said that Jesus has risen from the dead!' I shouted for the others while I fumbled to fasten my sandals.

'That's not all,' continued Mary. 'I saw Jesus. He spoke to me. He said he will meet you all in Galilee.'

'Are you sure he wants to meet me?' I asked, remembering my denial of him.

'He said all of you.'

'James! John!' I shouted, running from the door, elated. 'Follow me. Quickly!'

We ran to the tomb. John, a faster runner, got there first, but he hesitated at the entrance.

When I arrived, panting, I brushed past John and went straight in. Mary was right. Jesus's body wasn't there. The cloth in which he had been wrapped was discarded, as if the body inside had simply melted away.

That evening I sent a message to the others in Bethany. They arrived in twos and threes. Only Thomas was missing. 'Lock the doors,' I told James. A strange calm descended. I looked up and saw Jesus in our midst. We fell down in awe and joy and worshipped him.

'Peace be with you,' said Jesus. 'As my father sent me as a teacher, so I send you. Teach people that I died for them. Tell them to trust me and to follow me. Be sure of this – I am with you always.'

We returned to Galilee. It was safer than Jerusalem. Over the next forty days Jesus appeared to us several times. One night, some of us were out on the lake, fishing. At dawn, disappointed with our empty nets, we headed back to shore.

'Have you caught anything?' called a man from the shore.

'Not a thing.'

'Cast your nets on the other side of the boat.'

We did as the man said. The nets were immediately filled with so many fish that we had difficulty pulling them in.

I realised who the man was.

'Jesus!' I cried, plunging into the water to swim to him. He had lit a fire, on which he was already cooking fish. He had bread too, which he broke in his familiar way and shared with us.

After our meal, Jesus asked me, 'Do you love me?'

'Yes Lord. You know that I love you.'

'Feed my sheep,' he commanded. I understood that he meant I should teach the people.

Later he asked me again, 'Do you love me?' and again I said I did.

Again he said, 'Feed my sheep.'

A third time he asked me. It reminded me of the three times I had denied knowing him. Sadly, I said, 'Lord, you know everything. You know that I love you.'

'Feed my sheep.' Then I understood. He had forgiven my denials of him. He spoke again. 'Peter, when you are old they will stretch out your hands, bind you, and take you to a place that you don't want to go to.'

This shocked me. He seemed to be saying that I would die in the same way he had died. It has taken me a long time to accept that this will be my eventual end. Meanwhile I have God's work to do.

The last time we saw Jesus, he again urged us to continue his work down here on earth. 'You will be filled with God's power,' he told us. 'John baptised people with water, but you will be baptised with the Holy Spirit.' He looked up, and started to rise from the ground – we watched in amazement as he slowly ascended, and continued watching until the clouds hid him from our view.

Then began a period of waiting.

The eleven of us remaining since Judas left met frequently to pray as a group, along with Mary Magdalene and Jesus's mother. Other believers joined us until we numbered over one hundred. We elected Matthias to take Judas's place.

As Jesus had promised, we were visited by the Holy Spirit. One day, we were all gathered together when a noise like a strong wind filled the house. We felt as though tongues of fire from heaven ignited us with the ability to speak in languages we had never spoken before. People from outside, hearing the noise, came to see what had happened. There were people from many countries. Each of them heard us in their own language. They were amazed.

The power of the Holy Spirit spoke through me to the crowds. 'God sent Jesus to be handed over to his enemies who crucified him. God raised Jesus from the dead. Jesus is Lord and Christ.'

I called on them to turn away from sin and be baptised. About three thousand people were baptised and joined us that day. Our numbers continued to grow, and many joined us in teaching, spreading the word of Jesus.

Some time later, a lame man begged money from me as I entered a temple with John.

'I have neither food nor money,' I replied, 'but I will give you what I have. In the name of Jesus Christ, get up and walk.' I helped him to stand, and he walked with us into the temple. Recognising him as the lame beggar, people were amazed.

'Why are you surprised?' I asked. 'We have done this in Jesus's name.' Many who heard me believed, but the temple guards were angry and arrested us.

The next day they took us before the priests who had helped to condemn Jesus. 'How did you heal the beggar?' they demanded.

We told them about Jesus and about the gift of the Holy Spirit. After discussing the matter in whispers, they warned us never again to speak about Jesus or teach in his name.

'Which is right, to obey you or to obey God?' I asked. 'We must speak of what we have seen and heard.'

Unsure what to do, and unable to deny that the lame man could now walk, they repeated their warning and set us free.

There were now about five thousand of us teaching about Jesus. The temple authorities felt increasingly threatened. Once again, they arrested some of us. That night an angel opened our prison doors. 'Go to the temple courts and teach,' he told us.

We did as he said. When the guards found us, we were surrounded by crowds. The guards led us quietly out. Once again I found myself standing before the council of priests. They were angry because we had ignored their warnings.

'We must obey God, not people,' I explained calmly.

'These people are trouble. We should kill them,' someone murmured.

A wise council member called Gamaliel advised the council to release us. 'If their purpose is of human origin, these people will fail,' he told them, 'but if their purpose is from God as they claim, you will find yourselves fighting against God: you will not win.'

Thanks to Gamaliel, we were whipped rather than killed. Although it was agonising, we felt honoured to suffer in God's name.

By now there were so many believers in Jesus that the twelve of us found them hard to manage. An unpleasant disagreement arose between two groups of believers about the distribution of food. I suggested that they should choose seven people to look after the believers' business affairs, which would leave us free to concentrate on preaching.

One of the men chosen was Stephen. He was a man richly blessed by God, and his face shone with virtue, but I think some people were jealous of his position. They bribed others to lie to the council that they had heard Stephen say that Jesus would destroy Jerusalem and change the law of Moses.

Stephen was accused of blasphemy, and summoned to appear before the council.

A friend who attended the trial told me that he spoke eloquently and at great length. 'Was there ever a prophet that you and your fathers did not persecute?' he challenged them. 'They even killed those who predicted the coming of Jesus. And now you have betrayed and murdered Jesus, who was the best of us all. You have received the law from angels, but have not obeyed it.'

What courage! Stephen must have known that this would anger the council. Of course, they were furious, but Stephen looked up to heaven and saw the glory of God. 'I see heaven,' he said, 'with Jesus standing at the right hand of God.'

The council members,
now furious, dragged
Stephen outside and
pushed him over the edge
of a cliff. The crowd threw
rocks down on him. As the
great stones broke his body,
Stephen prayed for God to
forgive those who threw them.
I mourned the loss of a good
man, a good friend. Will I have such courage when
my time comes?

Stephen's death marked the beginning of the
persecution of the followers of Jesus in Jerusalem.
A man named Saul was particularly influential in
persecuting us. He was responsible for many cruel
deaths.

We fled, travelling far and wide. We taught and
healed wherever we went, spreading the good

news that Jesus had died in order to show us a new way to God. One day, having secretly met up in Jerusalem, we heard strange news from Damascus. Saul, our main persecutor, was claiming to have seen the risen Christ. He was bravely preaching Jesus's message, and had changed his name to Paul.

Can we trust him? we wondered.

Paul's preaching eventually brought him to Jerusalem. He was looking for us. Was this a trick? Could we trust him?

'He has preached fearlessly in Jesus's name,' argued Barnabas. 'We must welcome him.'

I felt my old uncertainty return. I wished that Jesus was there to tell me what to do. I decided that I had to trust God. When Paul knocked on our door, I opened it

wide. 'Welcome, Paul.' My trust was rewarded.
Paul became a good friend and ally.

With Paul on our side, our lives became safer.
I continued to travel. One afternoon, in Joppa,
I had gone onto a flat roof to find quiet and to
pray. In my prayer, I saw a vision in which a
sheet was lowered from heaven, containing all
kinds of animals, reptiles and birds – creatures
we would not normally eat. Then a voice said,
'Get up, Peter. Kill and eat.'

'Surely not, Lord!' I replied, 'I have never
eaten anything impure or unclean.'

The voice answered, 'Do not call anything
impure that God has declared clean.'

This happened three times in all. Then the
voice said, 'Now, Peter, three men are waiting
for you downstairs. Go with them.'

I went downstairs. The men worked for a
Roman centurion called Cornelius, who had

told them to bring
me to him. We left
the next morning.
When we
reached his
house, Cornelius
knelt at my
feet. I felt
embarrassed. 'Get up. I am only a man, like
you,' I said. I now understood the meaning of
my vision.

I explained to Cornelius, 'By our law, a Jew is
not allowed to associate with non-Jews, but God
has shown me that Jesus and his teaching are
for all people.' We talked about Jesus's life and
death and about his teachings. Everything was
now clear to me. I agreed to baptise these men,
even though they were Romans.

When I returned to Jerusalem my friends
criticised my actions, but when I described my
vision, they praised God. 'Peter, you were right

to give Romans the opportunity to repent and turn to Jesus,' said Philip.

King Herod, the ruler of Judea, was becoming nervous of our growing influence. He might be Jewish, but he worked for the Romans, and wanted to please them. He began another persecution.

First James was tried and executed, and then I was arrested again. I was heavily guarded and chained. One night, in a dream, an angel came to me. 'Get up and follow me,' he said. My chains fell off, the prison gate opened, and I walked past the guards. When I woke up, I really was free. Wrapping my cloak around my face to avoid recognition, I hurried to a house in which many of my friends were gathered. I knocked softly until they let me in. I told them what had happened, and then fled. Herod's men would soon come looking for me.

Inside, I am still Simon the fisherman. Although Jesus named me Peter and gave me strength, purpose and understanding, I still experience my old uncertainties. I've now spent half of my life teaching, healing, and fleeing persecution. I'm growing weary, but my work is not finished.

There are divisions amongst our people. They argue over how freely we can reinterpret Jewish law. I don't know the answer, but others have strong opinions. Worried, I travel and talk to various groups. 'Discuss calmly,' I urge, 'respect each other's opinions.' As often happens with anyone trying to keep the peace, I seem to attract anger from both sides.

The number of believers continues to increase. Paul has sent news that there are even believers in Rome. He has done well. He is a fearless preacher. However, not all news from Rome is good. Believers there are being persecuted for refusing to worship the Emperor as a god. Our believers in Rome have asked for our support.

'Peter, you should go,' my friends insisted yesterday. 'You are the most experienced. You knew Jesus best.'

'I am tired,' I replied. 'Choose a younger man instead.'

Yesterday I thought this was the right decision. Today is different.

Last night I dreamed that I was running away from Rome, frightened. I saw Jesus, hurrying in the opposite direction, towards Rome. I called out to him, 'Lord, where are you going?'

Without stopping he called back, 'Since you are leaving my sheep, I am going to Rome to be crucified again in your place.'

I stopped. Still in my dream, I turned round and began to walk back to Rome.

Now I know I must go to Rome. Although I am certain I am travelling towards the death that Jesus once predicted for me, I will not deny him this time. I am not afraid.

TAKING THINGS FURTHER
The real read

This *Real Reads* volume of *Simon Peter* is our
interpretation of the events of the New Testament,
told from the perspective of one of the most
important participants. In writing this account of
Simon Peter's life, we have used evidence from
both the gospel according to Matthew and Acts of
the Apostles. Matthew's gospel is one of the four
gospels – the first four books of the New Testament.

It is important to acknowledge that all four of the
gospels were written after Jesus's death, and that
the writers had different aims in mind – although
they all wanted to engender faith in the reader that
Jesus was the Son of God. The first three gospels –
Matthew, Mark and Luke – are called 'the synoptic
gospels'. They were probably written between forty
and sixty years after the crucifixion. The gospel
according to John, written later, is significantly
different.

Sometimes, the four gospels' accounts of events
differ considerably. At first this made our task rather

difficult, until we realised that what we needed to do was present the New Testament as it is, rather than to weave a path of our choice between the gospels. Therefore, if you read all six books in the *Real Reads* New Testament series, you may well notice some of the apparent contradictions and inconsistencies that are present in the Bible itself.

For the latter part of Simon Peter's life, we have drawn on evidence from Acts of the Apostles. Many people think Acts was written by the same Luke who wrote Luke's gospel, some time between 60 and 70 CE. The writer probably knew both Simon Peter and Paul.

Simon Peter did not write down his own thoughts and experiences, so we do not know what he thought of the events through which he lived. Using thorough research and paying close attention to the Bible account, we have tried to imagine what he might have been like, and what he might have thought.

This *Real Reads Simon Peter* does not cover all the events of the New Testament. Reading the other five books in the series will bring you closer to an understanding of the complete story. You may then want to read the New Testament itself. We recommend that you read either the *New International Version* or *The Youth Bible*, details of which are given below.

Biblical sources

On the *Real Reads* website you will find an online concordance (www.realreads.co.uk/ newtestament/concordance/simonpeter). A 'bible concordance' is an indexing tool which allows you to see how the same words, sentences and passages appear in different versions and translations of the Bible. This online concordance will direct you from events in the *Real Reads* version back to their biblical sources, so you can see clearly where each part of our story is drawn from. Although *Simon Peter* is based on the story as told in the gospel of Matthew and Acts, there are a few places where we have drawn on other sources.

Life in
New Testament times

The main events of Simon Peter's life with Jesus took place in Palestine, a long narrow area of land bordered to the west by the Mediterranean Sea and to the east by the Transjordanian Desert. Some parts of Palestine were desert, some were hill country, some rich pasture land, and some uncultivated wilderness.

Although Palestine was Jewish land, it was part of the Roman Empire and under Roman control. The Jews resented paying taxes to Rome. During Simon Peter's lifetime, there was considerable conflict between the Jews and their Roman rulers. This helps to explain why the Romans might have been nervous of the crowds following Jesus.

The Jews considered Palestine to be their 'promised land', promised to them by God. Moses had led them there from slavery in Egypt. The area was mainly Jewish, with synagogues and temples. Nevertheless, it is interesting that

most of Jesus's ministry took place around the Sea of Galilee, an area with a mixed population of Jews and Gentiles, and a reputation for political unrest. This is the area in which Simon Peter and his brother Andrew grew up.

Simon Peter lived in Capernaum, on the shores of the Sea of Galilee. Capernaum was a fishing town and a thriving commercial centre. Before he followed Jesus, Simon Peter had a secure living as a fisherman. During Jesus's ministry, the disciples based themselves in Capernaum, probably in Simon Peter's home. After Jesus's death, Simon Peter travelled widely and became a leader of the emerging Christian church.

Like most people, Simon Peter would have lived in a quite basic house built of mud or stone. The routines of people's lives followed the seasons as many were involved in agriculture, herding goats and sheep, or fishing. The area around the lake was quite fertile, growing a range of fruit, grain and vegetables. Fish and bread were staples of their diet.

Simon Peter was Jewish. Jews of the time, as is still the case for many orthodox Jews today, followed very strict laws. The Old Testament tells the story of how these laws, the Torah, were handed down from God to Moses. It must have been strange for Simon Peter when Jesus seemed to challenge the Torah.

Finding out more

We recommend the following books and websites to gain a greater understanding of the New Testament.

Books

We strongly recommend that you read the rest of the *Real Reads* New Testament series, as the six narratives interlock to give a more complete picture of events. These are *Jesus of Nazareth*, *Mary of Galilee*, *Judas Iscariot*, *Mary Magdalene* and *Paul of Tarsus*.

● *New Century Youth Bible*, Authentic Lifestyle, 2007.

● *Simon Peter: The Training Years* and *Simon Peter: Challenging Times*, Helen Clark, Day One Publications (Pocket Bible People), 2009.

● *People in the Life of Jesus*, Colin Lumsden, Day One Publications, 2003.

Websites

- www.bbc.co.uk/religion/religions/christianity
Lots of information about Jesus, history and the Christian faith.

- www.localhistories.org/new.html
Brief but useful descriptions of many aspects of everyday life in New Testament times.

- www.biblepath.com/peter
Brief but very accessible information to Simon Peter.

TV and film

- *Jesus of Nazareth* (1977), directed by Franco Zeffirelli. ITV DVD. A six-and-a-half-hour mini series.

- *The Miracle Maker* (2000), directed by Hayes, Sokolov. ICON Home Entertainment. Animation.

- *The Parables of Jesus* (2006), Boulevard Entertainment.

- *He is Risen* (2006), Boulevard Entertainment. A 30-minute animation about the resurrection and the meaning of Easter.

Food for thought

Here are some things to think about if you are reading *Simon Peter* alone, and ideas for discussion if you are reading it with friends.

Starting points

- Simon Peter doesn't hesitate when Jesus asks him to follow. Why do you think this is? How do you think this fits with the often-heard advice not to follow strangers?

- Simon Peter asks many questions. Write a list of his questions and the answers he receives.

- Simon Peter makes many mistakes. Can you find some of them? Why do you think Jesus chooses him to be his 'rock'? What qualities do you think Jesus recognises in him?

- On several occasions, Jesus tells people to serve others. Can you find some of these?

- Why do you think Simon Peter denies knowing Jesus? How does he feel about this afterwards?

- Can you find evidence that Simon Peter begins to take on a leadership role immediately after Jesus's death?

- What change occurs in Simon Peter when the Holy Spirit enters him? Can you remember any times when you have suddenly gained confidence?

Group activities

- With a group of friends, choose some important scenes from the book and act them out. What advice would you give to the person playing Simon Peter?

- Talk to your friends about times when you have made mistakes. What did you learn from your mistakes? What do you think Jesus feels about Simon Peter's mistakes?

- Talk about friendship together. Draw up a list of qualities you look for in a friend. How many of these qualities does Simon Peter possess?

MARY
OF GALILEE

www.realreads.co.uk

Retold by Alan Moore and Gill Tavner
Illustrated by Karen Donnelly

Published by Real Reads Ltd
Stroud, Gloucestershire, UK
www.realreads.co.uk

ISBN 978-1-906230-25-8

Printed in China by Imago Ltd
Designed by Lucy Guenot
Typeset by Bookcraft Ltd, Stroud, Gloucestershire

CONTENTS

THE CHARACTERS

Mary

God has chosen Mary to be the mother of his son. What will this mean for her?

Joseph

Engaged to Mary, Joseph too has responsibility for the young Jesus. What can he teach him?

Elizabeth and Zechariah

Elizabeth and Zechariah think they are too old to have children, until an angel visits Zechariah. Who will their son become?

4

Jesus

Jesus is the Son of God, but he
is also Mary's son. How will the
events of his life
affect his mother?

John the Baptist

John is preparing the way for
someone special – who is it?

Simon Peter

A loyal friend to Jesus. Can he
help Mary through events no
mother should experience?

Mary Magdalene

One of Jesus's closest friends.
What experiences will she share
with Jesus's mother?

5

MARY OF GALILEE

My son. Even now those words swell my aging heart with love before wringing it with agony. I want to shout his name from the rooftops; I want to curl up tightly and weep. Oh, my son.

You've probably heard stories of his birth, his life and his death. Can you spare the time to listen to my account? I should like to tell the whole story, just once, before I die. You needn't worry that the swiftly-passing years might have diminished my memory. How could incidents of such intensity ever fade? Every day of my life I live with the physical pain and motherly joy of the beginning, and with the maternal agony and spiritual reward of the end.

I'm sure I'm not the only person to have wondered why God chose me. I still wonder. I was an ordinary Jewish girl from an ordinary, happy family.

My parents were good people who kept the Lord's commandments. We loved God, we loved each other, and we loved our life in the Galilean village of Nazareth. I also loved Joseph, a craftsman, who had recently asked me to marry him. As I said, ordinary. Nothing unusual.

Do you believe in angels? I think I had always believed in them, but that didn't make it any less of a shock when one appeared before me. I must have been about fourteen years old when it happened. I was alone in the house, sewing, when the quality of the light seemed to change. I squinted up from my close work. As my eyes gradually adjusted, I saw a man, or at least a being, all in white, suffused with the purest light you can imagine. You ask me how I felt? Afraid, of course.

The angel smiled. 'Do not be afraid. The Lord is with you.' I stared, transfixed. His voice was gentle. 'Mary, you have pleased God.

You will soon be with child. You will give birth to a son, and you will name him Jesus. He will be called the Son of the Most High, and his kingdom will never end.'

My mind span so quickly that I felt dizzy. 'How can this happen?' My voice must have been a terrified squeak. 'I am unmarried, a virgin.'

'The Holy Spirit will come upon you, and the power of the Most High will overshadow you, so the holy one to be born will be called the Son of God.'

'The Son of God?' I gasped.

The angel, who told me his name was Gabriel, hadn't finished. 'Your relative Elizabeth is also going to have a child,' he continued. 'She is already in her sixth month of pregnancy.'

I was astonished. Elizabeth had never been able to have children, and now she was an old woman.

'Nothing is impossible with God,' asserted Gabriel.

In spite of everything, I trusted his words. 'I am the Lord's servant,' I replied. 'May it be as you have said.'

My parents supported me. They suggested that I visit Elizabeth, who lived with her husband in the Judean hills. As I approached, I saw her outside her house and called out to her. Giving an astonished cry, she put her hands on her rounded belly. 'Mary!' She rushed towards me. 'Mary! As soon as I heard your voice the baby in my womb leapt with joy. Blessed are you among women, and blessed is the child you bear. Why am I so favoured that the mother of the Son of God should visit me?'

'How do you know I'm pregnant?' I asked in wonder. 'And how do you know who my baby is?'

Elizabeth led me inside. 'Sit down and rest,' she smiled. 'I'll explain.'

I looked at her kind, aging face, blooming with the promise of motherhood. 'I think it's you who should rest,' I said.

Elizabeth's husband, Zechariah, had followed us inside. He silently beckoned to us both to sit down, then went to prepare some drinks.

'I'm afraid Zechariah can't speak,' explained Elizabeth. 'An angel told him that he would not be able to speak again until our son is born.'

Zechariah came back into the room, and nodded ruefully. I sat forward in my seat. This story promised to be as strange as my own.

'Six months ago,' began Elizabeth, 'Zechariah was on duty in the temple. He had been chosen from amongst the other priests to go into the inner temple and burn incense.'

'How did he tell you this if he can't speak?'

'He wrote it down,' explained Elizabeth. 'Mary, did an angel visit you?' she asked me. I nodded. 'Then you'll be able to imagine how Zechariah felt when an angel appeared beside the altar.' I nodded again. 'The angel told him not to be afraid, that our years of prayer had been answered. He said that I would bear a son, and that we must call him John.' Elizabeth chuckled. 'I wish I could have seen Zechariah's face. The angel told him that God will love our son and fill him with the Holy Spirit.' Elizabeth's face had grown more serious. 'John is supposed to bring Jewish hearts back to God and bring disobedient people back to righteousness. He has to prepare our people for someone who is to follow.' She looked at my own belly, which was not yet showing signs of the child growing within it.

'But why can't Zechariah speak?' I asked.

'Poor man,' smiled Elizabeth. 'He angered the angel by asking him how he could be sure. "I am Gabriel," the angel scolded him. "God sent me to tell you this good news. Because you doubted God's words, you will be unable to speak until your son is born."'

Zechariah went to fetch our drinks. Placing them on the table, he indicated that we should all join hands, then he looked expectantly at me. The need to praise God bubbled within me, and the words erupted from me. 'My soul praises the Lord, and my spirit rejoices in God my saviour, for he has recognised our humble status. From now on all generations will call us blessed, for the mighty one has done great things for us. Holy is his name! His mercy extends to all those who fear him. He has performed mighty deeds, he has scattered those who are proud. He has brought down rulers from their thrones and has raised the humble. He has filled the hungry with food, but the rich he has sent away empty. He has helped our people, remembering to be merciful to the descendants of Abraham forever, just as he promised.'

I stayed with Elizabeth for three months, returning home just before her son was born. She later told me that Zechariah's voice didn't return immediately. On the day of John's circumcision, Elizabeth's neighbours said, 'You should call him Zechariah, after his father.'

'I'm not going to call him Zechariah,' Elizabeth replied.

'What do you want to call him?'

'John.'

'John?' they exclaimed. 'But you have no relatives called John! What about tradition?'

They called on Zechariah to name the baby, handing him a stone tablet to write upon. 'His name is John,' he wrote. Immediately, he was able to speak again. 'His name is John.'

Years later, Zechariah described having felt the same urge to praise God that I had experienced. 'Praise be to the Lord,' he remembered shouting, as soon as his voice returned. 'He has saved his people from our enemies and from the hand of all who hate us. He will show mercy and enable us to serve him without fear in holiness and righteousness forever.' Raising his new son towards heaven, he blessed him. 'You, my child, will be called a prophet of the most high; for you will prepare the way for the Lord. You will teach people that they will be saved by the forgiveness of their sins, because of the tender mercy of our God. The rising sun will come to us from heaven to shine on those living in darkness, to guide our feet into the path of peace.'

People wondered at this for many months. What was this baby going to do? Meanwhile John quietly began the job of growing up, until it was time for him to play his very important role.

As I said, I was engaged to be married to Joseph. Joseph was a good man and was quite understandably upset when I told him that I was pregnant. He knew without a doubt that he was not the father. How could he marry me? The angel Gabriel appeared to Joseph in a dream and explained everything. The wedding could go ahead as planned.

In the final month of my pregnancy, the emperor, Augustus, wanted to know how many people lived in the Roman world, and what property we owned. He therefore ordered a population census. Every man had to register himself and his family in the town from which his family originated. Joseph was of the line of David, so we had to go to David's city – Bethlehem.

Joseph and I were anxious. The journey would be long, particularly as we would need to avoid the dangers of hostile Samaria. For additional safety, we decided to travel with others making the same journey. Once Joseph had managed to find a donkey for me to ride, we set off.

God protected us. We arrived in Bethlehem about a week after leaving home. It was evening and we were travel-weary. 'We'll never find a room,' I fretted. Bethlehem was packed with visitors registering for the census.

Joseph knocked on the doors of several homes, but their guest rooms were all full. We tried to trust that God would care for us, but we couldn't help worrying. Finally, our prayers were answered. 'The only space I have is where the animals sleep,' apologised a kindly householder, looking pityingly at me. 'You are welcome to stay there. It will be warm, and I changed the straw this morning.'

And so my first child, the Son of God, was born amongst the cattle. It was frightening. I was young and far from home. I longed for my mother, but our host's kind wife helped me. As soon as I heard my son's first cry and held my beautiful boy in my arms, I forgot the fear and pain and wept with joy. I fed him and wrapped him tightly in strips of cloth to keep him secure and warm. When Joseph finally persuaded me that I needed to sleep, I laid Jesus in a manger, the frame that held the animals' hay.

In the small hours of the morning, Joseph gently woke me. I thought my baby must need feeding, but through my bleary eyes I saw that he was sleeping peacefully. 'What is it?' I asked Joseph.

'We have visitors.'

I looked up to see three men, dressed in the warm, rough clothes of shepherds. 'Shalom,' they greeted me. 'We're sorry to disturb your sleep, but we must greet the saviour.' Looking a little embarrassed, one of them explained, 'An angel came to us while we were watching over our sheep.' When I told him that I recognised his description of the angel he continued with greater confidence. 'We were terrified,' he admitted, 'but the angel said that he brought great news.'

Another shepherd took over the tale. 'The angel told us that a baby had just been born in Bethlehem. He said the baby would be a saviour.'

'He said we would find him lying in a manger,' smiled the first shepherd, looking over at Jesus. Then he turned his gaze upon me, his eyes still dazed by what he had experienced. 'Other angels appeared, singing – lots of them.

It was beautiful. They sang, "Glory to God in the highest, and on earth peace to those who have pleased him."'

The shepherds knelt in silence next to my sleeping boy. As dawn broke, they took their leave of us. I knew that they would tell everybody they met all that had happened that night.

These events still hold a firm place in my heart and mind. I ponder them now as I pondered them then. My son. A saviour.

When Jesus was eight days old we followed Jewish custom and took him to the temple in Jerusalem to dedicate him to God and make our sacrifices. We had to pass through the city on our journey home.

When we arrived at the temple, a holy man approached us, wonder in his eyes. 'My name is Simeon,' he told me, his voice trembling with emotion. 'May I hold your baby?' With Jesus in his arms, his voice grew steady and loud. 'Sovereign Lord, you promised that I would not die before I had seen your son. You can now dismiss me in peace, for I have seen the salvation you have prepared for all people.'

Simeon's words attracted attention from others. They stared as he continued, 'This child will change many things. There will be conflict. Many will speak against him.' Then, looking kindly at me, he said softly, 'And a sword will pierce your own soul too.' This made me shiver. The image was painful, but what did he mean by 'too'? How much was my son going to suffer?

A very old lady, a prophetess, tapped me on the elbow. Quietly, she answered some of the questions in my heart. I was so young, so innocent. I had so much to think about.

I also had a baby to care for. Any mother will tell you how busy your first child keeps you. Any mother will also tell you that anxiety settles upon your soul like an uninvited guest you fear will never leave. And most mothers haven't been visited by angels and warned of their child's frightening future! However, most of the time, like all mothers, I managed to push my fear aside and enjoy Jesus's childhood.

Jesus was a wonderful son. Of course, he could be mischievous and playful, like any child, but I have years of happy memories which I often summon to comfort my old age.

Joseph and I tried to be good parents. We taught our children the scriptures and Jewish law. Every year, our family travelled to Jerusalem to celebrate the Passover feast.

Although the journey was long, we made it safer and more enjoyable by travelling with friends and relatives. It was an annual family holiday.

One year, when Jesus was twelve, we lost him. Having enjoyed a wonderful Passover, Joseph and I relaxed as we and our friends left Jerusalem for the journey home. We assumed that Jesus was somewhere in the crowd of travellers. He was a sensible boy. We never worried that he would do anything silly. At the end of our first day's journey, we started to look for him. 'Sorry – haven't seen him all day,' people told us.

'We'll have to go back into the city,' said Joseph, worried. As soon as the sun rose the next morning, Joseph and I turned back. We searched everywhere except for the most obvious place. We asked everybody we saw whether they had seen a twelve-year-old boy, alone. We were growing quite frantic when a priest approached us. 'There's a boy in the temple,' he said. 'Could he be your son?'

'Of course! The temple!' How could we have
failed to think of that? 'Is he well?' asked Joseph.

'Very well indeed. That's quite a boy you've got
there! He understands the scriptures better than
some of us who've been studying them all our
lives!'

We hurried to the temple, where we found
Jesus talking to a group of men on the steps. We
probably embarrassed him by rushing towards him,
full of the anger that accompanies a parent's relief.

He politely excused himself from the men and led us away. 'Did you not know that I must be about my father's business?' he asked, genuinely puzzled.

I feared that this might mark the turning point, when Jesus would assume the responsibilities for which he had been born. You can probably understand my relief when this didn't seem to be the case. Although he began to study the scriptures even more avidly than before, and he certainly prayed more often, he still seemed content to play with his friends and learn practical skills from Joseph. Nevertheless, there was a focus deep within him, a sense of purpose that I could never reach.

The years passed and little changed. When Jesus was in his late twenties, I noticed that he was growing restless, but still he stayed at home. I wondered whether he was waiting for a sign that his work should begin. If so, what would the sign be? Did he know?

Elizabeth and Zechariah visited us. John had left home some time ago. Elizabeth smiled fondly, but a little sadly, when she described how he had become a wandering prophet, living in the wilderness and baptising people in the River Jordan. 'They call him John the Baptist,' Zechariah added, putting his arm around Elizabeth's shoulders. Jesus listened with interest.

'Perhaps you should go to John,' I suggested to Jesus. What would have happened if I hadn't said that? Would he have gone anyway? Would he still be alive today? Would God's word have gone unheard?

Jesus was unusual. When he wanted to do something, he didn't discuss it endlessly like many people. He prayed, reached a decision, and acted upon it. That's what he did that night. Instead of sleeping, he spent the night in fervent prayer. The following morning, he announced, 'I am going to John.' After a brief farewell, he left.

I suppose that was the day I lost my son. It was a painful parting for me. When Jesus did eventually return to Nazareth, he was a changed man. No longer the son I had known, I suppose he was his true self – God's son. Explaining to me the significance of his baptism by John, he said, 'I have come to bring people back to God. That day with John was the beginning of my mission.'

In Jesus's absence, I kept myself busy with the usual duties of a wife and mother, but he was always in my mind. Eventually, we heard news that he and a group of men were travelling from village to village, teaching people to love

God and to love each other. When I enquired about their welfare, I learned that they had nothing; that they relied on people's generosity for food and shelter. Although I felt a mother's concern, I trusted Jesus's judgement.

Before long, Nazareth was buzzing with talk about Jesus. 'He heals the sick,' one neighbour told me. 'Yes, I heard that he made a blind person see,' added another. I even heard that he had made lame people walk, and had restored dead people to life. Some thought he had lost his mind, but I didn't doubt any of the things I heard.

Jesus and his friends were using a house in Capernaum, on the shore of the Sea of Galilee, as a base. Even though Capernaum was only a day's walk from Nazareth, many months passed before Jesus returned and introduced us to his friends. I liked them all – especially Simon. A fisherman by trade, he was a hard-working man who seemed devoted to Jesus. It reassured me to know that Jesus had such a man amongst his friends.

When Jesus did eventually return to Nazareth he came to teach rather than to visit. People were bursting with curiosity, and the synagogue was bursting at the seams.

Jesus was spellbinding. You might smile to hear me speak so fondly, but it is true. As he read the words of the Prophet Isaiah, we listened in awed silence. 'The spirit of the Lord is upon me,' he read. 'He has anointed me to bring good news to the poor. He has sent me to proclaim freedom for prisoners and sight for the blind, to release the oppressed.' I remember the light in Jesus's eyes. 'Today this scripture is fulfilled in your hearing.' There were surprised gasps; people looked at him in admiration. I also heard a low murmur amongst some. 'Isn't he just Mary's son?'

'You probably want me to heal people here, in my home town, just as you have heard that I did in Capernaum,' Jesus said to them. Many nodded. His reply disappointed them. 'People in other villages didn't know who I was, so they needed signs. But you have known me all my life. You should understand my words.'

The murmuring I had noticed earlier grew louder, the words more distinct. 'Is he saying that he won't help us? Are there no miracles for us in Nazareth?' Men rose to their feet, moving threateningly towards Jesus.

I watched in horror as burly men bustled Jesus out of the

synagogue. They pushed him towards the edge of the cliff on which Nazareth is built. Terrified, I caught at people's clothes, begging and pleading with them to spare him.

'Shove him over the edge,' someone shouted.

They had Jesus right at the edge of a cliff. I held my breath, but Jesus was unafraid. He looked them in the eye, moved their hands aside, and passed back through the crowd. As he reached the safety of the village he turned back to them and said, 'No prophet is accepted in his home town.'

I was deeply shaken. Did he meet such hostility everywhere he went?

Jesus's work brought him in our direction only a few more times, when he would fill our small house with his friends. I understood why people were so drawn to him; he was a wonderful person to be with. When he talked with you, he gave you his full attention, as though his mind was empty

of everything but you. This wasn't just with me, his mother; he did this with everybody, whether old friends or strangers. Do you think that is a sign of perfect love?

Occasionally I managed to join Jesus for a few days, but I felt overwhelmed by the crowds. His teaching was simple: we should love God, and we should love each other as God loves us.

Jesus understood the way people thought. He could see the gaps in their commitment to God, the obstacles that stood in their way, and he was not afraid to bring them to people's attention. For most people, this was helpful. They went away with a new sense of purpose. However, there are always those who are resistant to the truth – particularly if it is an unwelcome truth about themselves. I saw with concern that he sometimes made enemies.

Some of these enemies were powerful men – our religious leaders, the Pharisees. They taught strict observance of the law, whereas Jesus taught that people should apply the law with love and compassion. He argued that the Pharisees sometimes forgot the loving intention of God's law. The Sadducees were even more powerful. They were the temple priests, often used by the Romans to uphold their laws. We look up to our religious leaders, having been taught this respect since childhood, and they have power over most aspects of our lives. Jesus argued that this power was being abused, that many of our leaders had become corrupt.

However, Jesus also continued to make many friends. He once introduced me to a group of wealthy women who, he said, provided enough financial support to make his work possible. One of them was Joanne, the wealthy wife of King Herod's steward. Another, Mary Magdalene, explained how she had met Jesus. 'He healed me,' she said simply. 'He drove out the dark demons of my life and showed me the light.'

I felt the interest that any mother would feel when her single, thirty-one-year-old son introduces a beautiful young woman. In hindsight, I can see that this rose from my weakness, a desire for my son to be safe, to be a family man. Jesus was so committed to his work that I doubt whether marriage ever crossed his mind. I also suspect that he knew that his life would be short.

When I look back, I realise that Jesus loved all of humanity equally, whether friends, enemies, or even family. As his family, we sometimes found this painful. Once, having not seen him for several months, we heard that he was preaching nearby. Jesus's brothers and I hurried to see him. 'Can you tell Jesus that we are here?' we eagerly asked a friend we recognised. I was later told that, upon hearing the message, Jesus had replied, 'Who is my mother?

My mother and brothers are those who hear God's words and put them into practice.' I understood that Jesus wasn't just mine any more. What Simeon had said was true. It felt as though a sword was piercing my heart.

There then followed a difficult time for us. Joseph suffered a long illness, his slow decline keeping us at home. I was still mourning his death when we heard the terrible news that Elizabeth's son John had been executed by King Herod. John had criticised Herod for marrying his brother's widow. I visited Elizabeth and we tried to console each other in our grief. I grew increasingly anxious for my own son in a dangerous world.

News of miraculous events continued to reach us. One story was that Jesus had fed five thousand people with just two fish and five loaves of bread. His healing ministry continued. As the revitalisation of our religion gathered pace, Jesus needed more help. He chose about seventy of his followers to travel the region preaching and healing. It was said that they, like Jesus, could cast out demons and heal the sick.

As you grow older, the years seem to pass more quickly. Passover seemed to come round sooner

every year. The year after Joseph died I looked
forward to it with less excitement than usual.
It would be the first time I had travelled to
Jerusalem without him. I planned to travel
with my children and friends as usual. Mary
Magdalene kindly helped me to cover the costs.

I hoped to meet Jesus in Jerusalem. He had been
moving slowly in that direction for some time,
continuing his ministry as he went.

Just after entering the
city walls, I found myself
chatting to somebody
who had recently seen
Jesus in Jericho. He
described to me how
people had lined the
streets, trying to catch a
glimpse of him. 'A tax
collector called Zaccheus

climbed a tree to see over the heads of those in front,' he laughed. I smiled as I listened. 'Jesus called out to Zaccheus that he wanted to stay in his house. Zaccheus almost fell out of the tree in astonishment.' I giggled. I knew that Jesus would have been pleased. Most people hate tax collectors, because they are usually corrupt. Jesus had shown the crowd what forgiveness means. Another man forgiven and accepted by God.

Our conversation was interrupted by a crescendo of noise. Men, women and children were running into the street, shouting, tearing down palm branches and laying them on the road. In the distance I could hear voices singing psalms of hope and praise. The singing came nearer. What was happening? The palm is our national emblem, so this felt like the beginning of an uprising, or at least a protest against Roman rule. I felt a terrible sense of foreboding.

'He's coming!' I heard somebody shout. Standing on my tiptoes, trying to see over people's heads, I was just able to catch a glimpse of a man riding a donkey into the city. It was exactly as the scriptures had promised. My sense of dread became more specific. My heart missed a beat. It was Jesus. As my son passed through the crowds, people joined the procession, which grew larger and louder. Never before had I experienced such crowds; never before had I experienced such emotion, either in myself or in others.

I noticed some Pharisees looking very anxious by the roadside. Were they concerned for their own positions, or were they concerned for all of these innocent people, daring to oppose the great might of Rome? I felt compelled to follow as Jesus led the crowd to the temple.

Reaching the temple court, Jesus stopped. The crowd stopped, holding its collective breath. For the first time in my life, I saw anger in my son's face. What was wrong? What would he do? 'This is it!' whispered a man to my left. 'This is the beginning of our freedom!' He must have been bitterly disappointed when, mastering his anger, Jesus gently dispersed the crowd.

The next morning I was near the temple when Jesus returned, his face firm with resolution. The scene greeting him was the same as the previous day. Money-lenders and tradesmen carried out their business of exploitation and corruption within the temple. Jesus and his friends marched in and caused chaos, overturning the tables of

the money-lenders and releasing sacrificial
animals. Jesus angrily accused people of
abusing God's house. More enemies. It was
now only a matter of time.

Jesus was busy, and I spent only an hour with
him on the afternoon of the Passover. When
the time came to say farewell, he held me tight.
It felt like goodbye. I went back to my lodging
and wept, waiting for news.

The next day, Simon
came to see me, deeply
troubled. He told me
everything that had
happened the
previous night. He
said that Judas, one
of Jesus's closest
friends, had
betrayed him to

44

the authorities. Jesus had been arrested. Simon
wanted to spare me the details of the flogging
Jesus had suffered, but I felt strong. Nevertheless,
the description sickened me. I trembled to think
of my beloved son alone in the hands of those
who hated him. How could they hurt a man who
taught only love and peace?

'Where are the others?' I asked Simon.

'In Bethany.'

'Are they safe?'

'I think so.'

'What will happen now?' I dreaded the answer.

Simon held my hand. 'This morning they
brought Jesus before Pilate, the Roman prefect. I
think Pilate recognised Jesus as a good man. He
gave the crowd the opportunity to save him, but
the priests had whipped the people into a frenzy.
They were almost hysterical.'

'So they didn't save him?' I held my breath.

'No.' He looked away from me. 'They're going
to crucify him. Today.'

I felt sick. I remembered the words of the holy man who had held Jesus as a baby: 'A sword will pierce your own soul.' I wanted to scream.

'Mary?' Simon was concerned.

I answered through my tears. 'Leave me now. I must pray.'

Alone, I knelt and begged God to save my son, to save his own son. At first I was desperate, but I gradually felt God's calming presence. This was the responsibility for which my son had been born. For some reason, I alone amongst women had been chosen to bear this agony. I felt the hand of God on my shoulder, reassuring me that I was strong enough. I had to be strong. I could do this. I knew I had to go to my son.

'Simon!'

He came back in, this time accompanied by John, another of Jesus's friends. John wore a hood pulled low over his face. 'John will take you to the Antonine fortress,' explained Simon. 'They will probably take Jesus from there to Golgotha.' Golgotha – the place of the skulls.

We didn't reach the fortress. It was too difficult to push our way through the crowds lining the streets. Some people wept, others were exulting. All fell silent as Jesus approached.

John held me tightly. Bleeding and bruised,

Jesus was dressed in an expensive robe which
was now stained with his blood. He was only
thirty-three, but he was bent like an old man
under the weight of the beam of his cross,
which he was forced to carry. I tried to catch
his attention, but though he did not meet my
eye I am sure that he felt my presence. I saw
Mary Magdalene and some of her friends in the
crowd following Jesus.

Exhausted, Jesus stumbled, and once fell
hard onto the ground. A guard lifted him
roughly to his feet, then seized a man from the
crowd. 'You carry his cross for him,' he growled.
I heard Jesus ask the man's name as they

shouldered the cross together. 'Simon,' answered
the man. 'I'm from Cyrene.'

'Thank you, Simon,' said Jesus. I wanted to
thank him too.

Simon's help restored Jesus a little. He found
the strength to turn to the group of weeping
women following him. 'Do not weep for me,' he
said, 'weep for yourselves and for your children.
The time will come when you will wish you had
never had children, for if people can do these
things, what more are they capable of?'

At Golgotha, soldiers took the beam and fixed it across an olive trunk. When they hammered the nails into my son's wrists and ankles I felt every blow as if it were my own flesh. It was the darkest time I have ever known.

Jesus spent his last hours on a cross between two criminals who were also being crucified. A mocking notice nailed above his head read, 'This is the King of the Jews.' People in the crowd at his feet taunted him, 'If you are God's chosen one, why don't you save yourself?'

Even in his extreme suffering, Jesus found it in his heart to pray for others. Looking down at those who had gambled over the clothes of which he had been stripped before being hung on the cross, he called out, 'Father forgive them, for they do not know what they are doing.'

One of the criminals dying beside Jesus shouted angrily, 'Aren't you the Christ? Save

yourself and us!' It was difficult for the dying men to talk. Hanging from their arms restricted their breathing and they could only gasp enough air to talk by lifting themselves on their nailed feet. The man on the other side of Jesus argued against the first. 'Don't you fear God, even now? You and I are punished justly, but this man Jesus has done no wrong.' Looking to Jesus, he pleaded, 'Remember me when you come into your kingdom.'

Jesus answered him, 'Today you will be with me in Paradise.'

I watched the life ebb from my son. Summoning his final strength, he pushed upwards on his feet and called out, 'Father, into your hands I commit my spirit.' They say the curtain in the temple tore in two at that moment. My son was dead. The world was as dark as night. The centurion in charge of the executions fell to his knees, exclaiming 'Surely this was a righteous man.'

I stayed at the foot of the cross, weeping with Mary Magdalene and other women who had loved Jesus.

Does time bring comfort? Can a mother ever recover from seeing her son in such agony?

We prepared his body for burial and laid him in the tomb that one of his followers had prepared. The following day, when Mary Magdalene visited the tomb, it was empty. She returned with the amazing news that Jesus might still be alive.

This news both astonished and comforted me. Jesus's resurrection brought new life and new hope for everybody. For many years now, Jesus's followers have continued his work in the face of great dangers. The movement that Jesus founded is spreading throughout many lands. I wonder how long it will take for Jesus's vision, a world filled with love, to be realised?

I understand now that Jesus's death brings hope, not despair. He has shown us the way to God, he has forgiven us all. That is what the angel meant. That is why Jesus was born, that is why he died.

I am old now, and my story is told.

One day soon, I shall be in Paradise with my son – my saviour.

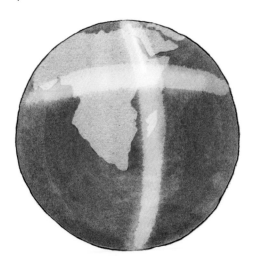

TAKING THINGS FURTHER

The real read

This *Real Reads* volume of *Mary of Galilee* is our interpretation of the events of the New Testament, told from the perspective of one of the most important participants. In writing this account of Mary's life, we have used evidence from the gospel according to Luke. This is one of the four gospels – the first four books of the New Testament.

It is important to acknowledge that all four gospels were written after Jesus's death, and that the writers had different aims in mind – although they all wanted to engender faith in the reader that Jesus was the Son of God. The first three gospels – Matthew, Mark and Luke – are called 'the synoptic gospels'. They were probably written between forty and sixty years after the crucifixion. The gospel according to John, written later, is significantly different.

Sometimes the four gospels' accounts of events differ considerably. At first this made our task rather difficult, until we realised that what we needed to do was present the New Testament as it is, rather than to weave a path of our choice between the gospels. Therefore, if you read all six books in the *Real Reads* New Testament series, you may well notice some of the apparent contradictions and inconsistencies that are present in the Bible itself.

In writing each of the six *Real Reads* New Testament books we chose a specific source to follow. To write Mary's account we chose Luke's gospel because it gives far more information about Mary and about the birth of Jesus than any of the other gospels. However, most people's understanding of the nativity is a combination of Luke and Matthew. Luke does not mention the visit of the wise men, or even the flight from King Herod. It is generally accepted that these were added to the birth story at a later date and for a particular purpose. As we have followed Luke's account, the wise men do not appear in the *Real Reads* version.

As far as we are aware, Mary did not record her

thoughts and experiences, so we do not know what she thought of the events through which she lived. Using thorough research and paying close attention to the Bible account, we have tried to imagine what she might have been like, and what she might have thought.

It is quite probable that Mary played a role in the development of the Christian church after Jesus's death. As his mother, she would almost certainly have visited his tomb. In Luke, we read that Mary Magdalene was in the company of other women at the tomb, but it does not specify Jesus's mother. We therefore made the decision not to include this in the *Real Reads Mary of Galilee*.

This version of Mary's story does not cover all the events of the New Testament. Reading the other five books in the series will bring you closer to an understanding of the complete story. You may then want to read the New Testament itself. We recommend that you read either the *New International Version* or *The Youth Bible*, details of which are given below.

Biblical sources

Although *Mary of Galilee* is based on the story as told in the gospel of Luke, there are places where we have drawn on other sources. On the *Real Reads* website you will find an online concordance (www.realreads.co.uk/newtestament/ concordance/maryofgalilee). A 'bible concordance' is an indexing tool which allows you to see how the same words, sentences and passages appear in different versions and translations of the Bible. This online concordance will direct you from events in the *Real Reads* version back to their biblical sources, so you can see clearly where each part of our story is drawn from.

Life in New Testament times

The main events of Mary's life took place in Palestine, a long narrow area of land bordered to the west by the Mediterranean Sea and to the east by the Transjordanian Desert. Some parts of Palestine were desert, some were hill country, some rich pasture land, and some uncultivated wilderness.

Although Palestine was Jewish land, it was part of the Roman Empire and under Roman control. The Jews resented paying taxes to Rome. During Jesus's lifetime, there was considerable conflict between the Jews and their Roman rulers. This helps to explain why the Romans might have been nervous of the crowds following Jesus.

The Jews considered Palestine to be their 'promised land', promised to them by God. Moses had led them there from slavery in Egypt. The area was mainly Jewish, with synagogues and temples. Nevertheless, it is interesting that most of Jesus's ministry took place around the Sea of Galilee, an area with a mixed population of Jews and Gentiles, and a reputation for political unrest.

Nazareth, where Jesus is commonly believed to have grown up, was a rather insignificant town – some argue that it did not even exist at that time. Mary and her family were probably quite poor. Although it is common belief that Joseph was a carpenter, it is more likely that he worked with stone than with wood. Most people lived in very basic houses built of mud or stone, often sharing part of their home with their animals.

The routines of life followed the seasons as many people were involved in agriculture. Most would have kept goats and sheep. The area was fertile, growing a range of fruit, grain and vegetables. Fish and bread were staples of their diet.

Jews of the time, as is still the case for many orthodox Jews today, followed very strict laws. The Old Testament tells the story of how these laws, the Torah, were handed down from God to Moses. Mary, Joseph and Jesus would all have had detailed knowledge of the Torah.

Finding out more

We recommend the following books and websites to gain a greater understanding of the New Testament.

Books

We strongly recommend that you read the rest of the *Real Reads New Testament* series, as the six narratives interlock to give a more complete picture of events. These are *Jesus of Nazareth*, *Simon Peter*, *Judas Iscariot*, *Mary Magdalene* and *Paul of Tarsus*.

- *New Century Youth Bible*, Authentic Lifestyle, 2007.

- *Mary: The Mother of Jesus*, Tomie dePaola Holiday House, 1995.

- *Just Like Mary*, Rosemarie Gortler and Donna Piscitelli, Our Sunday Visitor, 2003.

- W. B. Yeats, *Mother of God*. A short poem, to be found in most Yeats anthologies.

Websites

- www.bibleplaces.com
Particularly interesting discussion and pictures relating to Bethlehem.

- www.localhistories.org/new.html
Brief but useful descriptions of many aspects of everyday life in New Testament times.

- www.bbc.co.uk/religion/religions/ christianity/history/virginmary
Interesting information and discussion.

TV and film

- *Jesus of Nazareth*, directed by Franco Zeffirelli, ITV DVD, 1977. A six and a half hour mini-series.

- *Nativity Story*, directed by Catherine Hardwicke, Entertainment in Video, 2007.

- *Silent Night: The story of the First Nativity*, Abbey Home Media, 2004. A short, lively animation, which includes the wise men and Herod.

Food for thought

Here are some things to think about if you are reading *Mary of Galilee* alone, or ideas for discussion if you are reading it with friends.

Starting points

- What differences do you notice between this version of Jesus's birth and the story with which you are probably more familiar?

- What role do angels play in Mary's story? How do you imagine it would be to be visited by an angel? What messages do you think angels might bring to the world today?

- Why might it be important for Christians that Jesus was born to a poor family?

- Can you tell the story of the night of Jesus's birth from the viewpoint of one of the shepherds?

- Can you find examples of times when Mary fears for Jesus's safety?

- When Mary looks back on Jesus's life, what do you think she understands about his death?

- Why do you think Mary is such an important person for many Christians?

Group activities

- With a group of friends, act out this version of the birth of Jesus. Stop at different points and interview Mary and Joseph about how they feel.

- As a group, find all the evidence you can that Mary was a loving mother to Jesus.

- Choose four important events from the story, taking it in turns to play the part of Mary. After each scene, interview the person playing Mary about their experience and feelings. You could turn these interviews into an interesting newspaper-style report.

JESUS OF NAZARETH

www.realreads.co.uk

Retold by Alan Moore and Gill Tavner
Illustrated by Karen Donnelly

Published by Real Reads Ltd
Stroud, Gloucestershire, UK
www.realreads.co.uk

ISBN 978-1-906230-24-1

Printed in China by Imago Ltd
Designed by Lucy Guenot
Typeset by Bookcraft Ltd, Stroud, Gloucestershire

CONTENTS

THE CHARACTERS

Jesus

As the Son of God, Jesus has been given an enormous task. What will this mean for him?

Mary and Joseph

They know that their son Jesus is special. How can they ensure that his childhood will prepare him for his future?

John the Baptist

Living in the wilderness, John's job is to prepare people for Jesus. How will he be rewarded for his work?

Mary Magdalene

When Jesus heals Mary, does he already know the role she will play in his work and in his life?

Simon Peter

Simon is a simple fisherman. What qualities does Jesus see in him? Will he let Jesus down or fulfil his hopes? Or both?

Judas

One of Jesus's twelve most trusted friends, what role will Judas play in his master's life?

Pharisees

Pharisees are men of God and men of the law. Why might they see Jesus as a threat? Will they listen to him?

5

JESUS OF NAZARETH

It wasn't until I went to see John the Baptist that I fully understood what my work was to be.

My childhood in Nazareth had been a happy one. I had friends, loving brothers and sisters and, of course, my mother and Joseph. My parents told me wonderful tales about my earliest days; I listened, fascinated, as their experiences became part of my identity.

As I grew older, Joseph taught me his trade. 'You'll need to earn a living one day,' he insisted.

Mary and Joseph were good Jews, observing the holy practices and teaching me the scriptures. The more I studied, the more these became my passion. 'I *need* to study and pray,' I tried to explain to my mother. 'I feel that I have an important job to do, even more important than Joseph's work.'

Mary looked concerned, but not surprised.

As I matured, my sense of purpose increased and my thoughts became more focused. All around me, people were making others' lives difficult. Those in greatest need of kindness, the sick and the poor, were often treated most cruelly. Some religious leaders created even more suffering by focusing on the law at the expense of compassion, or by exacting money from the poor. Surely this wasn't God's plan. Surely somebody needed to address these injustices.

I was still living at home when, just before my thirtieth birthday, a relative called Elizabeth visited us. She was concerned about her son. 'People call him John the Baptist,' she smiled. 'He's living rough in the wilderness south of Galilee, washing and baptising people in the River Jordan.'

We Jews were accustomed to ritual cleansing, but John was also urging people to change the way they lived, just as the prophets of long ago had taught. 'He claims to be preparing the way for somebody greater than him,' Elizabeth continued, 'somebody who will baptise us with the Holy Spirit and with fire.'

I remember the way my mother looked at me then. I saw sadness in her eyes as she whispered, 'You should visit him.'

Feeling a strong desire to be cleansed and present myself anew to God, I decided to walk the dusty miles to the verdant banks of the Jordan, where I found John.

'I've come to be baptised,' I said.

'I've been expecting you,' he greeted me, 'but surely it is *you* who should be baptising *me*.' I wondered what he meant.

As John submerged me in the cold river, I felt unexpected warmth in my heart. I suddenly saw all creation overflowing with God's love, and my heart was filled with a desperate love for everything.

As I burst joyfully out of the water,
the heavens opened to me,
and I heard a voice thunder,
'You are my son, with
whom I am well
pleased!'

I knew then for certain that I was the man
for whom John had been preparing the people. I
was God's son. This was the role for which I had
spent my life preparing.

My joy was soon replaced by fear and doubt.
The Son of God? What could that possibly
mean? What responsibilities did it carry?

Sons usually continued their father's work. As Joseph's son, I had continued his trade. My task now was to do God's work on earth.

Needing solitude, I walked away from the river and into the desert. I stayed in that barren place for many weeks, praying for guidance, asking God what he wanted me to do.

I had come without any food, and soon grew hungry. An evil voice, which seemed to come from outside my own self, suggested that as the Son of God I had enough power to turn the stones around me into food.

'Go on – try it,' urged the voice.

Though I was tempted, I knew this would be the wrong use of my power. I needed to pray, not think about food. I stopped worrying about my stomach, and it stopped nagging me.

So how *did* God want me to use my power? What *was* I capable of doing?

The hissing voice returned. 'Hey, Son of God, throw yourself from this cliff. You'll be fine – God will save you.'

'I already trust God. I don't need to test him.'

'Then show the people how powerful God is,' insisted the voice. 'Be a king, rule in his name.'

'No!' I shouted. 'No! People cannot be forced to love God!' The hissing voice was silenced.

There was only one way to do God's work. I had to give up everything. Modestly, selflessly and tirelessly, I had to show people how to love God, and how to treat each other. Whatever it might take, I had to make it possible for them to know – and to reach – God. Although I was afraid of where this might lead me, I knew that God would guide me.

I had been given a simple but enormous task. Leaving the desert, I walked for days towards the Sea of Galilee. Looking around me, I was pained more than ever by cruelty, injustice and greed. People thought that wealth was a blessing from God and, afraid of poverty, they clung to their possessions rather than sharing.

It wasn't only the poor who suffered. The sick were shunned, cast out from their villages and their families. People were afraid of sickness – they believed it was a punishment for sin.

In one town I saw the familiar sight of a lame beggar lying in the dust, his flesh covered with sores. Although he was begging for food, everybody walked straight past him. I had to act.

I challenged the passers-by. 'Aren't you ashamed to ignore this man's suffering?'

One man glanced in my direction. 'Please give him some food,' I pleaded.

The man hesitated, yet knelt with me beside the beggar. Touching the lame man, I felt God's power pass through me. 'Your sins are forgiven,' I breathed. I knew that God had given me the authority to forgive sin, but it must have been a strange thing to hear.

Trembling, the beggar stood up, his eyes widening as his sores healed. I too was trembling. Both men stared at me.

'How can you forgive sins?' marvelled the healed beggar. 'Only God can do that.'

Ignoring the question, I turned to the other man. 'Feed him as you would want to be fed if you were hungry.'

'Yes,' he replied, clearly moved. 'I will.'

God had granted me his love and courage to transform lives, and to bring people back to him. I continued to travel around Galilee, healing people and pleading with them to love each other.

Although my message was simple, many struggled to understand. As word spread about my work, the crowds grew larger. There were so many people with so many needs – I couldn't do this alone. 'Father,' I prayed, 'please send me the help I need.'

Early one evening I arrived on the Bethsaida shore of Galilee, where I noticed two fishermen casting their nets into the sea. I called out to them. They immediately drew in their nets and hurried towards me. They were brothers, Andrew and Simon.

We ate together, and as we talked I realised that God had answered my prayer. 'Come with me,' I said, 'and I will make you fishers of people.'

After a brief pause first Simon, then Andrew, stood up and followed me along the shore. We met two more fishermen brothers, James and John. I knew that God wanted them to help me too. They were working with their father at the time, but without hesitation they left him and followed me.

The five of us walked into Capernaum, where Simon and Andrew welcomed us into their home. My friends, being plain, honest fishermen, were able to talk to the local people in a way that was easily understood. God had chosen well.

God needed me to speak wherever people gathered, so I visited synagogues and taught from the scriptures. One such afternoon, a man burst into the synagogue. 'What do you want, Jesus of Nazareth?' he shrieked. 'Have you come to destroy us?'

I heard people around me murmur that he was possessed by an evil spirit. I placed my hand on the man. 'Come out of him!' I commanded the spirit. The poor man fell screaming to the floor, and then was perfectly calm.

'Who are you?' somebody asked in awe. 'Even evil spirits obey you.'

In the early days it was easy to find the peace and quiet I needed to pray, to gather my strength, and to think ahead. But news travels faster than human feet, and soon I could no longer enter a village without a crowd surrounding me. Sometimes I yearned to escape, and my friends tried to protect me, but still the people flocked.

I saw in their faces that their need for
compassion was far greater than my need for
rest. Some were despairing, some angry. Many
were lost. I knew what it was to be human, to
feel lost and afraid. How could I turn anybody
away? Can any shepherd turn his back on a lost
lamb?

In spite of their poverty, people provided
us with food and shelter. In one village
God sent me Mary Magdalene,
a woman who was deeply
troubled and desperately
wanted to be healed.

With God's help I was able to heal her, and from then on Mary supported our work. She had money of her own, which she gladly offered to help us to be more effective in God's service.

Teachers of Jewish law often visited us at Simon's house, which had become our base.

One such afternoon I was explaining the nature of forgiveness. 'Surely only God can forgive sins,' one teacher fretted.

Outside, we could hear the familiar sounds of a crowd gathering. We tried to continue our discussion, but after a while were distracted by sounds above us. Simon leapt to his feet. 'They're breaking through my roof!' he cried. It was true – we looked up and saw daylight.

When the hole was large enough, a sleeping mat, suspended on ropes, was slowly lowered. On the mat lay a man. 'He is paralysed, Rabbi,' a voice called from the roof.

'But we know that you can heal him.'

I felt their faith move within me as I knelt beside the man and took his hand. 'Your sins are forgiven,' I said quietly.

Some of the teachers gasped. I sensed their disapproval even before they spoke. Who was I, a mere man, to forgive people's sins? Saddened by their inflexibility and lack of compassion, I turned to the paralysed man. 'Take up your mat and go home.'

Amazed, the man tested the strength of his legs. Standing tentatively, he rolled up his mat and thanked me. His friends on the roof cheered.

Some of the teachers were perturbed. Having spent their lives studying and rigidly applying the laws given by Moses, it was difficult for them to understand the true nature of God's love. I wished they could understand that people must forgive each other, just as God will always find a way to forgive us.

Whenever I healed someone I was accused of blasphemy against God. It seemed so hard to show people that God's law is about love and forgiveness. What would it take?

I found myself in unwelcome conflict over another issue too.

Jewish law states that the Sabbath must be a holy day, free from work. It's a sensible law, guaranteeing us space in each week to think about what God wants of us, rather than concentrating on the day-to-day concerns of our lives. Unfortunately, though, many teachers placed too much emphasis on the Sabbath's restrictions and rules, rather than on its opportunities for rest and reflection.

One Sabbath, as I entered the synagogue, I saw a man with a withered hand. A tense silence descended. People watched intently, waiting to see whether I would heal him on the Sabbath.

'Stand up,' I urged the nervous man. Then I turned to the people. 'Which is lawful on the Sabbath,' I asked them, 'to do good or to do evil?'

Nobody said a word.

Here was an opportunity for me to demonstrate both God's compassion and his authority.

I turned back to the man. 'Stretch out your hand.'

As he held out his trembling hand, it began to grow and fill. He moved it around. He clenched and unclenched his fist. Most people gasped, but some remained stony-faced. I knew then that there were people who would try to stop my work. Most people, however, wanted to be guided towards living a good life. They wanted to be pure before God.

The crowds following me continued to grow. Sometimes it was difficult to address so many people. I often stood on higher ground to talk, so that more might see and hear.

When teaching by the lakeside, I used to take a boat onto the water and speak from there.

How could I reach more people? I realised that I needed to choose some special people from amongst my closest followers, people who could help me spread the message.

I chose twelve. In Simon the fisherman I saw a man who, in spite of his mistakes – perhaps because of them – could be a rock on which I could build the future. I called him Peter, meaning 'rock'. I also chose his brother Andrew.

I nicknamed James and John 'the sons of thunder' because of their powerful preaching.

The others I chose were Philip, Bartholomew, Matthew, Thomas, James bar Alpheus, Thaddeus, another Simon, and Judas Iscariot. To Judas, an educated, conscientious man, I gave responsibility for the group's money.

Before these men could teach and heal, they still had much to learn. I had to prepare them. 'Tell people stories, or parables,' I advised them. 'If we simply repeat the laws, they'll follow them rigidly. Parables help people to apply God's law to their lives. We have to help them to understand God's message in a way that makes sense to them.'

I explained how important it was for the twelve to set a good example. 'Be generous; don't hide the light of God's love. If you show love and compassion, others will learn from you. Like seed sown on good soil, the word of God, sown by you, will produce a crop a hundred times what was

sown. The seeds will grow and multiply without
you having to do any more work. This is what God's
kingdom is like. We must create the kingdom of
God on earth.'

I faced a difficult dilemma. I needed to reach
as many people as possible, but I was reluctant
to draw attention to myself. The Romans ruled
our country with a reasonably gentle hand, often
cooperating with the Jewish authorities. I didn't
want to threaten them. I wasn't seeking conflict.

Though I frequently asked people not to talk
too much about the things we did, people gathered
in large groups to hear what we had to say, and
people needing help continued to seek us out.
Having crossed the lake one day, I was greeted
on the shore by another crowd, led by Jairus, a
synagogue elder. He was deeply distressed.

'My daughter is dying,' he wept. 'Please heal
her.'

As I followed Jairus through the crowd, I suddenly felt a familiar healing flow of love. I stopped and looked round. 'Who touched the fringe of my robe?' I asked. It must have seemed a strange question in the midst of a jostling crowd.

A woman edged forward. 'I'm so sorry,' her voice trembled, 'it was me. I've been ill for years and no doctor has been able to help me.'

'Daughter, your faith has healed you,' I said. 'Go in peace.'

As we approached Jairus' house, two men ran out. 'Jairus, we're so sorry. She is dead!'

'Don't be afraid,' I reassured Jairus. 'Believe.'

Jairus led me to where his daughter lay. Taking her hand, I spoke to her gently. 'Talitha koum. Little lamb, arise.'

The child opened her eyes, stood up, and walked over to her mother. I asked those within the house to tell nobody what had happened. With such a large, anxious crowd waiting outside, however, there was little chance of that.

I hadn't visited my family in Nazareth for almost two years. It was time to return.

My family welcomed me. That Sabbath, in the familiar synagogue, I read aloud from the scriptures. My former friends and neighbours listened in silence. A chill breeze of resentment whispered to me from the crowd, making me shiver. It warned of approaching storms.

Later, in the street, two men confronted me. 'Who do you think you are?' one of them challenged. 'You're just a craftsman, Mary's son!' More men gathered.

I was astonished by their hostility. I reminded myself that a prophet is never welcomed in his own town. Saddened, I walked through the angry crowd. Nobody tried to stop me.

More sadness was to follow. News reached us that John the Baptist had been beheaded under King Herod's orders. Herod was a God-fearing man, but he was weak. Although he had recognised John's virtue, he had feared his power and influence. He had surrendered to his fear. I grieved both for John and for Herod.

We were living in dangerous times, but God's work had to be done. My twelve friends were now ready for their important task. I sent them off in pairs so they could support each other. 'You are now my apostles, my disciples. You have God's authority to preach and to heal,' I told them. 'Take nothing with you; God will provide everything you need.'

Several weeks later the twelve returned, tired but elated. We tried to find a secluded place down by the shore so we could share our experiences without being disturbed by crowds of people, but it was impossible. The people, like lost sheep looking for their shepherd, followed us. I loved them, and could not ignore them. That evening, we fed all five thousand.

At nightfall I advised the apostles to take the boat out on the lake. I would join them later. When I eventually found them, a storm was blowing. Though their fear sometimes exposed weaknesses in their faith, I learned that they had done their work well.

The following morning we sailed across Galilee to Gennesaret, where we taught and healed for several days. While we were there, we were constantly and openly watched by a group of Pharisees, strict teachers of the law. They often came over to talk with us and challenge us.

One day we stopped to eat in the market. Hungry and tired, we were enjoying a brief respite from the crowds. My heart sank when I saw a group of frowning Pharisees approaching. One man, who had been particularly confrontational in previous conversations, cleared his throat. 'Ahem. Why didn't you carry out the ritual cleansing before you ate?'

I sighed. 'Nothing can make us impure just by going into our body,' I explained.

We were attracting attention, and a small group gathered round us. 'This food, coming from the outside, will pass through our stomachs and come out again.' Someone laughed. 'It is the things that come from the inside – our thoughts and feelings – which have the power to make us clean or unclean.'

I was beginning to understand that my work would not be complete until I had sacrificed my life, as was foretold in the scriptures. By sacrificing me, his own son, God would prove that there is nothing that can separate people from his love.

Seeking closeness to God, I took Simon Peter, James and John to a mountaintop to pray. I felt God's presence there more intensely than ever before – it reminded me of my baptism in the Jordan. As I prayed, I was enlightened with deeper understanding. Moses and Elijah appeared beside me and, as at my baptism, I heard God's voice saying 'This is my beloved son.'

Later, as we descended the mountain, I knew what I had to do.

Although my disciples were good men, their faith and understanding sometimes failed them. Sensing that my time on earth was limited, I occasionally felt frustrated by them, the kind of frustration a loving parent experiences towards their child. 'How much longer must I be with you?' I once asked. And, like children, they sometimes argued amongst themselves about who was the most important. 'The one who wants to be the greatest must learn to be the servant of all,' I reminded them.

In their concern to shield me from crowds, the disciples once tried to usher away a group of women who had brought their children to be blessed. I stopped them. 'Let the children come,' I said. 'The kingdom of God belongs to such as these.'

Unsophisticated, dependent, innocent, and willing to learn – that is how we should all be before God.

A little later a young man, clearly wealthy, approached me. 'Teacher,' he asked, 'what must I do to enter God's kingdom?'

I smiled. He genuinely wanted to do God's will but, as for so many people, an obstacle stood between him and God. His obstacle was his wealth. 'Sell everything you have and give it to the poor,' I advised him. 'Then follow me.'

The man's face fell. He couldn't do it. He turned dejectedly and walked away. That night I prayed for him.

As I explained to the disciples, 'It is impossible for the rich to enter the kingdom of Heaven. You must forsake everything.'

'We have forsaken everything,' said Simon Peter anxiously.

'And you shall have your reward,' I reassured him. I didn't tell him how much he would have to suffer before he received it.

Our journey was leading us relentlessly towards Jerusalem, towards confrontation. It was time to prepare my disciples for what lay ahead.

'In Jerusalem I will be betrayed to the chief priests.' They listened quietly. 'They will condemn me to death. People will mock, flog, and kill me. Three days later I will rise from the dead.' The men were pale and silent.

The time for quiet reasoning and diplomacy had run out. Did this mean I had failed? Many people had heard my message and believed, others were still trying. However, the religious and political authorities were making people's lives ever more difficult. Significant change now called for significant action.

I rode into Jerusalem on a colt, as predicted in the scriptures. A crowd followed. More crowds gathered along the way to welcome me, singing psalms of expectation. 'Hosanna in the highest!' they called, as they tore down palm

branches and laid them before my colt's feet.
The palm was a national emblem, a symbol of
Jewish unity. A threat.

'They welcome you as a king!' observed
Simon Peter. The disciples were excited. Some
of them had been longing for this action. They
thought we were finally challenging the right
of the Romans to rule over us; even that we
were challenging the Jewish authorities. But
the true purpose of what lay ahead was far
greater than any of them could imagine.

'Blessed is he who comes in the name of the Lord!' shouted the crowd. 'Blessed is the coming kingdom!'

Our work in Jerusalem had begun. I led the procession to the temple to pray but, dismayed by what I found there, I asked the crowd to disperse, and took the disciples out of Jerusalem. We would return tomorrow.

A temple is supposed to be a peaceful place, where people can hear God's voice. Instead of peace, however, we had encountered a cacophony of moneychangers and people selling animals for sacrifice. Traders were using the temple court as a short cut as they crossed the city, bartering as they went. In what was supposed to be a place of prayer and contemplation, God's voice was being drowned out by the din.

The following morning, at the entrance to the temple, I saw a tough-looking man trying to exact temple tax from a weeping woman. Furious, I overturned his table. The disciples followed my lead, turning over tables and benches, causing chaos.

I had to make people see what they were doing. From the top of the steps I called out, 'It is written, "my house will be called a house of prayer for all nations", but *you* have turned it into a den of thieves!'

The chief priests were angry and afraid. They knew we were right.

The next day we returned to the temple, where people were now praying peacefully. A group of priests and elders confronted us. 'What authority do you have to do these things?' they asked.

Of course, I had God's authority, but I was aware that they were looking for an opportunity to accuse me of blasphemy. I refused to answer.

Challenges like this became more frequent and more hostile. I recognised fear in the faces of my challengers, the fear that would lead to my death. They tried to trap me in their webs of words. How sad they made me feel. Sad and tired.

'Teacher, you are a man of integrity,' began one young man, keen to try his wit. 'Tell us, should we pay taxes to Caesar or not?'

I must have sighed, for he smiled, thinking he had scored a significant victory. If I answered that they should not pay taxes to Rome, I could be arrested for sedition. If I advised them to pay taxes, the oppressed would probably reject me and my ideas.

'Why are you trying to trap me?' I asked. 'Show me a denarius.' I held up the coin. 'Whose portrait is this?' We all knew that it was Caesar's, and that the inscription on the coin proclaimed him a god. As this broke one of our commandments, Roman coins were deeply offensive to Jews.

'Why, it is Caesar,' answered my young challenger.

'Then give to Caesar what is Caesar's, and give to God what is God's. God doesn't need our money, he needs our hearts.'

Not all questions were hostile. One Pharisee asked me, 'Which is the most important of the commandments?'

I could see that he was a good man. 'The most important commandment is this,' I replied, 'that you love God with all your heart, with all your soul, with all your mind, and with all your strength. The second is this: love your neighbour as yourself.'

My questioner smiled. 'Rabbi, you are right. To love God and to love each other is more important than anything else.'

I smiled. 'You are not far from the kingdom of God,' I told him.

Though we visited the temple daily, our base at the time was outside Jerusalem, in the village of Bethany. One evening we were relaxing after dinner when a woman entered the room, carrying a long-necked alabaster jar filled with expensive perfume. Breaking the neck of the jar, she poured some of the perfume over my head.

'What a waste!' exclaimed Judas.

'She should have sold the perfume and given the money to the poor.'

Poor Judas. After three years of being responsible for our money, his reaction was natural. 'She has done a beautiful thing,' I corrected him. 'The poor will always be with you. You can help them any time, but you will not always have me. She poured perfume over me to prepare me for my burial.'

The disciples shuffled uncomfortably.

It was Passover, the greatest celebration of the Jewish calendar. Some of the disciples went ahead into Jerusalem to find and prepare a room for our meal. Although I had tried to warn them of what lay ahead, they did not realise just how soon the real trouble would begin. This was to be the last meal we would share together.

After a rather sombre meal together, we reclined in silence at the table. Although the mood was melancholy, we were physically and spiritually very close. It was time for me to address a difficult issue. These poor men.

'My friends,' I began, 'very soon one of you will betray me.' I knew that the betrayal was already under way, and I knew who it was.

Disbelieving, the men sat up. The closeness we had been enjoying just seconds before was replaced by suspicion and fear. 'Surely it is not me!' some exclaimed. 'Who is it?'

'It is one who dips bread into the bowl with me.'

Judas, who was dipping his bread into my bowl at that moment, swiftly drew back his hand. I wondered if any of the others had noticed.

It was necessary for God's plan that somebody should betray me, but it was a dreadful responsibility to bear.

Judas looked ashen. From this moment on, his life would be unbearable. In the confusion that followed, Judas rose weakly from his seat and left the room.

There was still work to be done. Picking up a loaf of bread, I thanked God and broke it. Passing it around, I said quietly, 'Take this; this is my body.' It symbolised all that I was; all that we had shared. Their faces were desperately unhappy. Some wept.

I picked up the wine cup. Again I thanked God and passed it among the eleven remaining disciples. 'This is my blood, God's new promise, poured out for you and for all people.'

They understood how important this promise was, but still did not fully comprehend what I had to do.

45

That night I went to the Mount of Olives to pray. My friends loyally accompanied me, but again I had to tell them a painful truth. 'Tonight, when they come for me, you will all run away.' To stay by my side would mean almost certain death. They were only human, after all.

Simon Peter was hurt and adamant. 'I won't leave you,' he insisted.

He was right. I knew he would never leave me, but his courage would have a limit. 'Tonight, before the cockerel crows twice,' I told him sadly, 'you will disown me three times.'

Tonight, more than ever before, I needed to pray for strength to endure the suffering that lay ahead. We walked to the garden at Gethsemane, my favourite place on the Mount. Leaving most of the men near the entrance to the garden, I took Peter, James and John with me. 'Stay here and keep watch,' I told them.

Having walked a short distance away from them, I fell to the ground, overwhelmed with sorrow. 'Father, you can do anything. If it is your will, take this cup of suffering from me.' My prayer was not answered. I did not find peace.

Returning to my friends, I found them sleeping. I felt terribly alone. 'Couldn't you keep watch for just one hour? You must stay awake!' Again I went to pray, but when I returned they had gone to sleep again. My grief was immense. My prayers were still unanswered.

On my third attempt I finally found God's calming presence. He gave me courage and peace of mind, and reminded me that this was the work for which I had been born. I found my friends asleep yet again. Reluctantly, I woke them. When I looked up, I saw Judas approaching with a group of armed men.

'Here comes my betrayer,' I said quietly,

Smiling, but ashamed to meet my eye, Judas greeted me and identified me with a kiss. I longed to comfort him, but there was no time. The guards seized me roughly. I tried to explain to them what they were doing, but they wouldn't listen.

As they led me away I accepted that the scriptures must be fulfilled. My disciples were nowhere to be seen.

The chief priest called his council together. There was never any doubt what the outcome of my trial would be. I pitied those who gave false evidence against me. Eventually the chief priest challenged me directly. 'Are you the Son of God?'

'I am,' I replied. 'You will see me sitting at God's right hand.'

'You heard the blasphemy!' he cried in triumph. He tore his clothes, a sign that he was condemning me to death.

I spotted Simon Peter hiding in the shadows, watching. My poor friend. What fear, what pain he must be suffering. Later I heard a cockerel crow twice, but I knew Simon Peter would never desert me. When I was no longer there he would be my rock, my foundation.

Early next morning they presented me to Pontius Pilate, the Roman prefect of the province. I sensed his discomfort as he questioned me. 'Are you the King of the Jews?'

I knew he wanted me to deny that I was, so he could release me, but I couldn't help him.

A crowd had gathered outside Pilate's palace. I was accustomed to crowds, but this one was different. Although I recognised some people in the sea of faces, many more were strangers, relishing the mounting hysteria. Priests prowled amongst the people, whispering, preparing them for their roles in the unfolding drama.

Pilate saw only one way to avoid responsibility. He handed the decision to the crowd, publicly washing his hands of his own guilt. 'What shall I do with the King of the Jews?' he asked.

At first just a few voices called, 'Crucify him!', but it soon grew into a loud, steady chant. 'Crucify him! Crucify him!'

'Why? What crime has he committed?' asked Pilate in disbelief.

The crowd continued chanting, baying for blood.

I was to be flogged and crucified. Unbearable suffering lay ahead. The brutal flogging would tear my flesh from my bones. People had died from these floggings alone. Later, they would drive iron spikes through my wrists, nailing me to a wooden beam. They would fix the beam to an olive trunk, driving another spike through my ankles. The sun's heat would be unbearable. When my damaged limbs could no longer support my weight, I would suffocate.

Experiencing human suffering through me – his own son – God would show that his love and forgiveness have no limits. Though I was weak and exhausted, I had to carry the beam for my own cross to a nearby cliff called Golgotha, 'the place of the skull'.

When I struggled under the weight of my beam, soldiers pulled a man from the crowd to help me. At Golgotha, other soldiers drove in the spikes. The agony made it hard to breathe,

hard to think, but I found the words to forgive. Then I prayed, trusting that people would finally understand and could start afresh. It was only my flesh that they hurt.

My final hours were long. As the end of my suffering drew near, I remembered a song to God from our scriptures, a psalm of despair and hope.

My God, why have you forsaken me? You are the holy one, the praise of Israel. Our fathers trusted you and were delivered, but I am scorned and despised by the people. All who see me mock me, saying 'He trusted in the Lord; let the Lord rescue him.'

From birth I was cast upon you; from my mother's womb you have been my God.

Do not be far from me, for trouble is near and there is no one to help.

I am poured out like water and all my bones are out of joint, my heart is like melted wax.

My throat is as dry as dust and my tongue sticks to the roof of my mouth.

You lay me in the dust of death.

People stare and gloat over me.

They divide my garments among them, and cast lots for my clothing.

Lord, do not be far from me.

Then my human suffering ended, but I was still in the world. I still had to explain to my friends that my death had opened up a new way to God for everyone. Only when they understood this would I be free to ascend to my father in heaven.

TAKING THINGS FURTHER
The real read

This *Real Reads* volume of *Jesus of Nazareth* is our interpretation of the events of the New Testament, told from the perspective of its most important participant. In writing this account of Jesus's life, we have used evidence from the gospel according to Mark. This is one of the four gospels – the first four books of the New Testament.

It is important to acknowledge that all four gospels were written after Jesus's death, and that the writers had different aims in mind – although they all wanted to engender faith in the reader that Jesus was the Son of God. The first three gospels – Matthew, Mark and Luke – are called 'the synoptic gospels'. They were probably written between forty and sixty years after the crucifixion. The gospel according to John, written later, is significantly different.

Sometimes, the four gospels' accounts of events differ considerably. At first this made our task rather difficult, until we realised that what we needed to do was present the New Testament as it is, rather than to weave a path of our choice between the gospels. Therefore, if you read all six books in the *Real Reads* New Testament series, you may well notice some of the apparent contradictions and inconsistencies that are present in the Bible itself.

In writing each of the six *Real Reads* New Testament books we chose a specific source to follow. To write Jesus's account of his life and ministry we used Mark's gospel, because it is widely considered to be the earliest of the gospels. We felt it is therefore most likely to be the closest to Jesus's actual words. We also feel that it gives the most personal and moving version of Jesus's death.

Jesus did not write down his own experiences, so we do not know what he thought of the events through which he lived. Using thorough research and paying close attention to the Bible account, we have tried to imagine what he might have been like, and what he might have thought.

This *Real Reads Jesus of Nazareth* does not cover all the events of the New Testament. Reading the other five books in the series will bring you closer to an understanding of the complete story. You may then want to read the New Testament itself. We recommend that you read either the *New International Version* or *The Youth Bible*, details of which are given below.

Biblical sources

On the *Real Reads* website you will find an online concordance (www.realreads.co.uk/ newtestament/concordance/jesus). A 'bible concordance' is an indexing tool which allows you to see how the same words, sentences and passages appear in different versions and translations of the Bible. This online concordance will direct you from events in the *Real Reads* version back to their biblical sources, so you can see clearly where each part of our story is drawn from. Although *Jesus of Nazareth* is based on the story as told in the gospel of Mark, there are a few places where we have drawn on other sources.

Life in
New Testament times

The main events of Jesus's life took place in Palestine, a long narrow area of land bordered to the west by the Mediterranean Sea and to the east by the Transjordanian Desert. Some parts of Palestine were desert, some were hill country, some rich pasture land, and some uncultivated wilderness.

Although Palestine was Jewish land, it was part of the Roman Empire and under Roman control. The Jews resented paying taxes to Rome. During Jesus's lifetime, there was considerable conflict between the Jews and their Roman rulers. This helps to explain why the Romans might have been nervous of the crowds following Jesus.

The Jews considered Palestine to be their 'promised land', promised to them by God. Moses had led them there from slavery in Egypt. The area was mainly Jewish, with synagogues and temples. Nevertheless, it is interesting that most of Jesus's ministry took place around the Sea of Galilee, an area with a mixed population of Jews and Gentiles, and a reputation for political unrest.

Bethsaida

Capernaum

Gennesaret

GALILEE

Nazareth

SEA
OF
GALILEE

PALESTINE

RIVER JORDAN

Jerusalem

Bethany

10   20 miles

DEAD
SEA

Nazareth, where Jesus is commonly believed to have grown up, was a rather insignificant town – some argue that it did not even exist at that time. Capernaum, however, where he chose to base his ministry, was a thriving commercial centre. Jerusalem was the religious and political capital of Palestine. It is surrounded by hills, one of which is the Mount of Olives.

Most people lived in very basic houses built of mud or stone, often sharing their homes with their animals. The routines of life followed the seasons as many people were involved in agriculture. Most would have kept goats and sheep. The area was quite fertile, growing a range of fruit, grain and vegetables. Fish and bread were staples of their diet.

Jews of the time, as is still the case for many orthodox Jews today, followed very strict laws. The Old Testament tells the story of how these laws, the Torah, were handed down from God to Moses. Pharisees were teachers of the law who felt responsible for ensuring that people kept the laws. They were very concerned when Jesus seemed to challenge the Torah.

Finding out more

We recommend the following books and websites to gain a greater understanding of the New Testament.

Books

We strongly recommend that you read the rest of the *Real Reads* New Testament series, as the six narratives interlock to give a more complete picture of events. These are *Mary of Galilee, Simon Peter, Judas Iscariot, Mary Magdalene* and *Paul of Tarsus*.

● *New Century Youth Bible*, Authentic Lifestyle, 2007.

● Sally Lloyd-Jones, *The Jesus Storybook Bible: Every Story Whispers his Name*, Zondervan, 2007.

● J. R. Porter, *Jesus Christ: The Jesus of History, The Christ of Faith*, Duncan Baird, 1999. The photographs in this book offer a fascinating view of Palestine.

Websites

- www.bbc.co.uk/religion/religions/christianity
Lots of information about Jesus, history, and the Christian faith.

- www.localhistories.org/new.html
Brief but useful descriptions of many aspects of everyday life in New Testament times.

- www.rejesus.co.uk
Lots of interesting information about Jesus.

TV and film

- *Jesus of Nazareth*, directed by Franco Zeffirelli. ITV DVD, 1977. A six and a half hour mini-series.

- *The Miracle Maker*, directed by Derek Hayes and Stanislav Sokolov, ICON Home Entertainment, 2000. Animation.

- *The Parables of Jesus*, Boulevard Entertainment, 2006.

Food for thought

Here are some things to think about if you are reading *Jesus of Nazareth* alone, and ideas for discussion if you are reading it with friends.

Starting points

● Why do you think John was baptising people? What did baptism mean to Jesus? Why do you think Christians still use baptism today?

● How do you think Jesus feels when he realises that he is God's son? How would you feel if you were given so much power and responsibility? What would you do? What does Jesus decide to do?

● Why do you think Jesus chose fishermen as his first disciples? What qualities do *you* look for in a friend?

● Why do you think the disciples wanted to send the children away (see page 34)? Why did Jesus particularly want to see the children? What did Jesus think adults could learn from children?

● Why do you think Jesus accepted that he had to die?

- Find as many instances as possible of Jesus teaching people how to behave. Write a list of his 'instructions'. How might Christians today apply these instructions to their own lives?

- Christians believe that Jesus was and is both human and divine. Can you find any examples of Jesus struggling to be both?

- Why do you think the cross is an important symbol for Christians?

Group activities

- With a group of friends, take the roles of Jesus and the other characters from the book, and act one of the main scenes.

- Talk about what Jesus's friends thought about him, what his enemies thought, and what Jesus said about himself.

- Roleplay the different people on the day Jesus entered Jerusalem – the crowds, the disciples, Jesus. Afterwards, discuss the characters' feelings.

- In your group, imagine what would happen if Jesus returned today. This could be the beginning of all sorts of exciting and imaginative activities!